ACKNOWLEDGEMENT

I would like to thank Professor Anthony M. Pasquariello of the University of Illinois, who offered constructive criticism and valuable suggestions during the course of my writing. Thanks are also due to the University of Illinois Research Board, which provided me with the necessary funds to complete my research in Spain and interview Juan Benet.

TABLE OF CONTENTS

INTRODUCTION

Juan Benet is one of those extraordinary persons who has successfully pursued two careers which demand contrasting levels of intuition, sensitivity and creative genius: namely, the scientific rigors of modern engineering versus the esthetic demands of creative writing. By his own admission Benet is a full-time engineer (a profession which he actively pursues and enjoys) while he insists that he is only a part time author. Yet since the publication of his first novel, *Volverás a Región*, in 1967, Benet has proven to be one of the most prolific writers in Spain.[1] Although the esoteric nature of his works --especially his novels-- has greatly limited his popular appeal, Benet is considered by most critics to be one of the major figures in the development of new alternatives for the contemporary Spanish novel. As Manuel Durán concludes in his study of Benet: "La nueva novela española ha nacido ya y está en pleno desarrollo."[2]

Born in Madrid in 1927, Benet falls chronologically into the group of writers commonly known as the Generation of 1950. Due primarily to their neorealistic orientation and *engagé* approach to literature, this group of writers, and the doctrines which they espoused, became the predominant literary force in Spain for nearly thirty years following the Spanish Civil War. Yet despite the chronological affiliation with these authors, Benet represents a direct antithesis to their fundamental literary canons. Although he wrote drama and prose during the 1950's, he published very little during this period. His first play, *Max* (1953), corresponds in general to the neorealistic doctrines of the time, but it is his first and only work which does so. Eight years later, Benet published his first collection of short stories, *Nunca llegarás a nada* (1961), which foreshadows the tone, style and thematic concerns which the author develops more intensely in

---

[1]For a complete list of works which Benet has published through June of 1975, consult the bibliography found at the end of this study.

[2]Manuel Durán, "Juan Benet y la nueva novela española," *Cuadernos Americanos*, Vol. 195, N° 4 (julio-agosto de 1974), 193-204.

his later short stories and novels. When examining this group of stories in retrospect, it is not difficult to perceive that, even at this early date, Benet rejects the neorealistic techniques and themes and possesses an innovative attitude toward literature. Since the early 1960's Benet has exercised both in theory and practice an artistic freedom which, by his own choice, has placed him on the margin of the literary currents of the time. As a result, he has been able to produce a highly personal, complex system of writing which utilizes a negative assessment of post-war realism as the principal point of departure.

Despite the large amount of critical attention which Benet has received in recent years, he stands firm in his position that writing is a pastime which he pursues only when he feels like doing so. He does not aspire to gain power or influence as a professional writer, and has recently rejected a lucrative contract from a leading Spanish publishing house. Clearly, however, Benet underestimates the impact and importance of his position in the evolution of the contemporary Spanish novel. Although he claims that, "no he pretendido nunca hacer grandes revoluciones con mis escritos,"[3] he is unable to minimize the innovative qualities which his novels exhibit. Although it is premature to define conclusively Benet's ultimate influence on the Spanish novel, the present study is intended to serve as a detailed investigation of each of Benet's five novels written to date. As a result, we will be able to determine the essential characteristics of Benet's novelistic art, and thereby demonstrate clearly the radical differences between Benet and the literary generation in which he has lived. In addition, I have analyzed Benet's general theory of literature as expressed in his two major books of essays, *La inspiración y el estilo* (1966) and *Puerta de tierra* (1970). It is not my intention, of course, to compare Benet's theory of literature to his own manner of writing fiction. Nevertheless, his concern with stylistic development and rejection of the realistic tendencies of both the nineteenth century and post-Civil War era in Spain, appear particularly relevant when viewed in light of his own novels.

---

[3]Juan Benet, Lecture delivered at the Fundación March, 4 June, 1975.

Methodology

A great many systems or theoretical models exist within the realm of contemporary criticism. Some, such as the psychoanalytic or Marxist approach to literature, attempt to impose a previously determined system of literary values and ideas upon all works of literature. Others, such as phenomenological or value criticism, use the work itself as a point of departure, but examine only limited aspects of it. Because of the reduced area of emphasis of such schools of thought, I have opted for an eclectic approach to the novels of Benet, with principal reliance upon Anglo-American New Criticism. In general terms, the New Critics regard the literary work as an object, a *thing*, with meaning independent of the reality external to it. Consequently, the literary work is viewed as an ideal system of norms that calls into existence in any age a coherent body of responses. This "coherent body of responses" refers to the norms which are intrinsic to the work and cannot be determined by a critical system which attempts to utilize an external frame of reference or point of departure. The emphasis, as T. S. Eliot would say, must be placed on the poem, not on the poet.

Since the primary purpose of the present study is to discover the basic elements which compose Benet's novels --and thereby discover the new literary orientation which Benet offers-- I have expanded my intrinsic analysis in certain instances with supplementary theories. For example, I have relied upon Freudian principles and terminology in order to explain the recurring conflict between instinct and reason which Benet portrays in all of his novels. This does not mean, however, that I am using a psychoanalytic approach, but rather that I am drawing metaphorically upon Freud in order to clarify the norms which Benet creates. In addition, I have referred throughout my study to certain writers who have influenced Benet, with particular emphasis placed on William Faulkner. Several fundamental similarities exist between the novels of Benet and Faulkner, since the latter played a prominent role in Benet's literary formation. My study is by no means intended to serve as a comparison between the two novelists, but I have indicated several points of contact between them.

I have studied Benet's novels in chronological order, based on the date of publication, in order to portray more accurately the similarities and differences among the novels as Benet has progressed as a writer. I have not studied Benet's theatre or short stories because, in addition to the problems of genre, I believe his importance as a writer is due primarily to his novels.

Finally, it must be noted that my study can only hope to serve as an introduction to this complex and difficult author. Benet is relatively young and certainly has a lengthy writing future. As Benet matures and changes so may his novels, and undoubtedly his influence on the contemporary Spanish novel will need re-examination and critical study.

THE POST-CIVIL WAR NOVEL IN SPAIN

In order to determine Juan Benet's role in what some critics have called "la nueva novela española," it will first be necessary to establish the literary background of contemporary Spanish prose fiction. The novel of the post-Civil War epoch in Spain has undergone significant changes in recent years, and the present chapter is an attempt to summarize this metamorphic process.

Literary critics and historians unanimously agree that during the two decades following the Civil War the Spanish novel developed profound "realistic" characteristics. Indeed, critics have invented more than a score of terms in their efforts to describe the phenomenon of post-war *realismo*: *realismo objetivo, realismo social, realismo moral, realismo de crítica social, realismo dialéctico, realismo histórico, realismo irónico, behaviorismo,* etc. However, investigators of literary history disagree concerning both the value and originality of this realistic trend in Spanish prose fiction. Julián Marías, for example, claims that, "Asistimos a una recaída del costumbrismo: insistencia en casos, tipos genéricos o ambientes; personajes elementalizados colocados en un plano que los hace bidimensionales."[1] Eugenio de Nora also asserts that post-war Spanish realism offers little originality: "Ni la orientación realista (iniciada independientemente entre nosotros... hacia 1930), ni el concepto de 'literatura comprometida' (actualizado por Sartre, pero corriente y en vigor con más o menos fuerza desde el romanticismo), ni la obsesión por los problemas sociales (apenas interrumpida desde fines del siglo pasado), son ninguna novedad: adoptando esos principios la promoción joven no hace sino reanudar una tradición viva, represtinándola y procurando separar la ganga del metal puro."[2]

Other critics, however, defend the realistic novel, and claim that it transcends nineteenth-century Realism. Antonio Iglesias

---

[1] Julián Marías, "Prólogo" to *La novelística de Camilo José Cela* by Paul Ilie (Madrid: Gredos, 1959), p. 23.

[2] Eugenio de Nora, *La novela española contemporánea*, 2nd ed. (Madrid: Gredos, 1970), Vol. III, p. 261.

Laguna insists that, "La generación de 1910-1920 no ha de ser calificada como meramente costumbrista.... No comparto el pesimismo de otros críticos: que la novela española actual carece de valor por atenerse generalmente a un realismo social que le resta trascendencia."[3] Gonzalo Sobejano also supports the notion that the post-war Spanish novel is distinct from the nineteenth-century novel: "...[es] nuevo porque sobrepasa la observación costumbrista y análisis descriptivo del siglo XIX mediante una voluntad de testimonio objetivo artísticamente concentrado y social e históricamente centrado."[4] Thus while critics share the view that realism is the essence of the post-war Spanish novel, they support diverse theories concerning its origins, development and literary value.

The reasons for the popularity of neorealism in the Spanish novel are not yet totally clear. Certainly, however, the war itself is a critical factor. From 1936 to 1939 few literary works of importance were published in Spain. More decisive, however, is the fact that many of the best novelists of Spain went into forced or self-imposed exile during or following the war. Rigorous censorship was also put into effect in 1939, as the Franco government sought to expurgate all non-conformist literature from Spanish soil. Thus the development of Spanish letters during this period was severely retarded, and by 1941 Spanish prose fiction was in a state of what José Corrales Egea has called "orfandad": "La ausencia de maestros, el desconocimiento de su obra, la imposibilidad de entroncar con la novela particular e intrasferible --dado su carácter eminentemente 'personalista'-- de los autores del 98 llevó a los nuevos novelistas de posguerra a dirigir sus miradas al exterior o a empalmar con la novela galdosiana."[5]

The question persists, however, why the authors of the post-war era, who were writing during a time which has been described by some critics as a literary vacuum, reverted to realism?

[3]Antonio Iglesias Laguna, *Treinta años de la novela española* (Madrid: Editorial Prensa Española, 1969), pp. 148-150.

[4]Gonzalo Sobejano, *Novela española de nuestro tiempo* (Madrid: Editorial Prensa Española, 1970), p. 16.

[5]José Corrales Egea, *La novela española actual* (Madrid: Cuadernos para el Diálogo, 1971), p. 29.

As Corrales Egea suggests (above), it was a "return" to Galdós, the most recent, accessible Spanish novelist. Juan Ignacio Ferreras also supports this view, and urges that the decade immediately following the war be designated a period of "realismo restaurador." That is, the novelists of the post-war era returned to the recurrent characteristic of a large portion of Spanish literature: realism. Ferreras insists that "Se trata de una novela indudablemente realista... se trata de continuar la línea más idealizada o decadente del realismo tradicional; se trata de no actualizarlo con problemáticas del momento."[6]

Another, and perhaps more accurate theory, is that the novelists of Spain resorted to realism as a vital means of examining the ruinous condition of their country after the war. Camilo José Cela poignantly suggests this proposition in his novel *La colmena*, first published in 1951. The action of the novel takes place in Madrid, in 1942, where the *madrileños* still suffer from the traumatic effects of the Civil War. More than three hundred characters appear in the novel and represent a cross section of a ruined society: poverty, hunger, prostitution, despair and *abulia*. In his novel Cela offers a comprehensive view of post-war Madrid and implicitly criticizes the oppressed society of the time. As he affirms in the prologue to the first edition of *La colmena*: "Mi novela *La colmena* no es otra cosa que un pálido reflejo, que una humilde sombra de la cotidiana, áspera, entrañable y dolorosa realidad."[7] As an effective means of changing society, however, Cela doubts the efficacy of his work: "Sé bien que *La colmena* es un grito en el desierto: es posible que incluso un grito no demasiado estridente o desgarrador. En este punto jamás me hice vanas ilusiones."[8] On the other hand, as an impetus for literary change in Spain, "*La colmena* abre la puerta que da paso al realismo selectivo de intención crítica en la literatura española."[9]

---

[6] Juan Ignacio Ferreras, *Tendencias de la novela española actual* (Paris: Ediciones Hispanoamericanas, 1970), p. 202.

[7] Camilo José Cela, *La colmena*, 9th ed. (Barcelona: Noguer, 1967), p. 9.

[8] Cela, p. 11.

[9] Pablo Gil Casado, *La novela social española* (Barcelona: Seix Barral, 1968), p. 10.

8

In a sense, the post-war writers were confronted with a Spain similar to that of the Generation of 98. As Eugenio de Nora notes: "...[es] una especie de 'segundo' 98 que explique y ponga al descubierto las raíces del nuevo desastre nacional que es, a sus ojos, el derrumbamiento de la República. La guerra mundial marca, en tanto, un compás de espera, e indirectamente, de esperanza en cuanto la marea antifascista occidental parece reforzar, al menos moralmente, sus posiciones."[10] The members of the Generation of 98, of course, examined and criticized the Spain of their time, but in contrast to the writers of the post-war period, rejected (with the exception of Baroja) the realistic tradition which preceded them.

Juan Goytisolo, one of the most important contemporary Spanish novelists, also supports the "social circumstances" position for the growth of post-war realism. In his book, *El furgón de cola*, he emphasizes censorship as a fundamental cause for the type of novel written during this period:

> Mientras los novelistas franceses escriben sus libros independientemente de la panorámica social en que les ha tocado vivir, los novelistas españoles --por el hecho de que su público no dispone de medios de información veraces respecto a los problemas con que se enfrenta el país-- responden a esa carencia de lectores trazando un cuadro lo más justo y equitativo posible de la realidad que contemplan. De este modo, la novela cumple en España con una función testimonial que en Francia corresponde a la prensa, y el futuro historiador de la sociedad española deberá apelar a ella si quiere reconstituir la vida cotidiana del país a través de la espesa cortina de humo y silencio de nuestros diarios.[11]

The term "neorrealismo" which, as we have seen, is the cornerstone of nearly all critical commentary on the contemporary Spanish novel, connotes a variety of meanings. Gonzalo Sobejano perhaps has defined most succinctly the meaning which best

[10]Eugenio de Nora, Vol. III, p. 63.
[11]Juan Goytisolo, *El furgón de cola* (Paris: Ruedo Ibérico, 1967), p. 34.

describes its use in post-war literary Spain: "...entendiendo por realismo la atención primordial a la realidad presente y concreta, a las circunstancias reales del tiempo y del lugar en que se vive.... Ser realista significa tomar esa realidad como fin de la obra de arte, y no como medio para llegar a éste."[12] During the decade of the 1940's this realistic attitude became increasingly prevalent among Spanish authors. The realistic novel developed sporadically, however, with such novels as Cela's "tremendista" narrative in *La familia de Pascual Duarte* (1942), and Carmen Laforet's existentialist *Nada* (1945). According to most critics, Cela's novel represents the rebirth of the Spanish novel after the Civil War. As José García López has affirmed, *"La familia de Pascual Duarte constituyó un verdadero escándalo literario...[y] tuvo la virtud de poner de manifiesto el tono insípido y convencional de buena parte de lo que se escribía en el momento."*[13]

Realism in Spanish prose fiction did not evolve as a literary movement until the group of writers known as the "Generation of 1950" gained prominence at mid-century. Influenced by the Italian neorealists of the 1930's, the American "Lost Generation," and assisted in their efforts by the increasing number of literary prizes awarded each year in Spain, novelists such as Juan Goytisolo, A. López Salinas, Rafael Sánchez Ferlosio, Carmen Martín Gaite, José Fernández Santos, Luis Goytisolo Gay, Alfonso Grosso and others achieved significant literary stature while sharing similar views concerning the nature of literature. Nearly all of these writers regarded the novel primarily as a means of communication, and aspired to reveal in their works the disastrous state of contemporary Spanish society. Their primary objective was to submerge the reader in his surrounding reality and thereby move him to act. The authors therefore strictly avoided abstract metaphysics and philosophizing, and desired to make their novels accessible to the reading public. As Corrales Egea remarks concerning the Generation of 1950: "Frente a la afirmación de que el arte y la literatura son perfectamente inúti-

[12]Gonzalo Sobejano, p. 16.

[13]José García López, *Historia de la literatura española*, 7th ed. (Barcelona: Vicens Vives, 1962), p. 676.

les (lo que justifica que la sociedad burguesa tolere al artista como a una brillante y divertida inutilidad), reivindican un puesto dentro --no al margen-- de la sociedad, como cualquier hombre, y no como criatura superflua, de lujo, cuya misión sea ver, oír y cantar."[14] As a result of the emergence of these writers, the decade of the 1950's brought into fruition the neorealistic Spanish novel.

The Generation of 1950 also exhibited similar attitudes toward novelistic technique. Experimentation with narrative point of view and structure, or the fragmentation of spatial and temporal elements were disregarded in favor of more traditional methods of writing. Simplicity was preferred to ornamentation and concrete expression was believed to be more important than metaphorical elusiveness. Furthermore, since the principal interest of these writers was to portray the surrounding reality as accurately as possible, their most common narrative approach was one of objectivity. The term "objective," however, must be regarded with caution, because it connotes two rather distinct attitudes toward the novel. As Ramón Buckley has shown, although both terms are included under the heading of realism, it is necessary to distinguish between "objetalismo" and "objetivismo."[15] The former refers to a process of reification in which the author is concerned only with observable, material objects of reality. The latter term, in contrast, designates the perspective of the narrator, not the objects which he perceives. An "objective" author, or a writer of "objective realism," is detached from the events which he narrates and attempts to create the illusion of "photographic objectivity." A writer of "objetalismo," however, may be (and frequently is) completely subjective in his vision of the world. As a narrator in a novel he relates only external objects and behavior, either from an objective, but most frequently from a personal point of view. Such is the case, for example, with many French new novelists. As Robbe-Grillet has asserted, "El *nouveau roman* no pretende otra cosa que una total subjetividad... sólo Dios puede ser objetivo. Mientras que en nuestros li-

[14]José Corrales Egea, pp. 59-60.

[15]Ramón Buckley, *Problemas formales en la novela española contemporánea* (Barcelona: Ediciones Península, 1968). See specifically pages 37-77.

bros, por el contrario, es un hombre el que ve, el que siente, el que imagina, un hombre situado en el espacio y en el tiempo, condicionado por sus pasiones, un hombre como tú y yo."[16]

In Spain this "objetalista" stance reached its fullest development with the behaviorist novel of the 1950's, in which only the external, observable actions of characters were portrayed, while introspection and psychological intimacy were avoided. Although several important behaviorist novels were written during the 1950's, the finest example is *El Jarama* (1955), by Rafael Sánchez Ferlosio.

El Jarama represents a significant point in the evolution of the post-war novel primarily because of its narrative perspective. It symbolizes the maximum development of both the "objetalista" and "objetivista" novel in Spain. The latter tendency is evident in *El Jarama* due to the almost total absence of narrative intrusion: the characters speak and act independently, and a majority of the novel consists of short dialogues which take place without interference from the narrator. Ferlosio's "objetalista" attitude is manifest in part from the numerous dialogues in the novel, but is revealed principally from the work's overall construction, in which characters are treated essentially as material objects. We view only their external behavior, and the author makes no attempt to portray psychological depth. By means of "reproducing" the observable words and acts of the characters, and by strictly avoiding narrative digressions, Ferlosio paints a detailed portrait of Spanish society in which persons' lives are filled with nothingness.[17]

Critics disagree on the precise moment when the novel of objective realism began to lose favor among Spanish novelists. A generally accepted time span is between the years 1958 and 1961. José Corrales Egea suggests that during this period the realistic novel bifurcates into two tendencies: 1) an intensification of objective realism represented by such novels as *Nuevas amistades*

---

[16]Cited in Buckley, p. 43.

[17]Although Ferlosio opts for an objective narrative point of view in the novel, the "objetalista" attitude is manifest in his method of viewing only external behavior in the portrayal of the characters.

(1959) and *Tormenta de verano* (1961) by Juan García Hortelano, and Juan Marsé's *Encerrados con un solo juguete* (1960). Portraying reality as a series of facts and events, authors of intensified objectivism make no attempt to synthesize or explicate in their role as narrator. 2) An attenuated realism in which the writer becomes more personally expressive, and plays a more central role in the novel, either through direct intervention or narrative manipulation. Novels which represent an increasingly mitigated realism include *La resaca* (1958) by Juan Goytisolo, *Central eléctrica* (1958) by López Pacheco and Alfonso Grosso's *La zanja* and *Un cielo difícilmente azul*, both published in 1961.[18] Although both tendencies co-existed during the late 1950's and early 1960's, the latter gained increasing importance, while the former decreased in popularity and influence.

The Spanish Novel of the 1960's

As we have seen previously, although the neorealistic novel did not grow extinct in Spain by 1960, there existed a growing awareness among both novelists and critics that it had run its course. Nonetheless, as late as 1962 in Paris and 1963 in Madrid, the social realists of the Generation of 1950 vehemently defended their *engagé* attitude toward the novel. In a series of interviews in *Les Lettres Français* of July, 1962, several important Spanish novelists declared their literary philosophy. Following are a few examples:

Juan Marsé: Il est bien connu que le premier devoir de tout romancier consiste à décrire la réalité sans la falsifier.... Mais, en outre écrire des romans, pour moi, c'est toujours défendre une cause.... La mission que je m'assigne dans notre société (et de la place d'écrivain que j'y occupe) est intimement liée aux circonstances politiques de cette société. (p. 5)

Alfonso Grosso: ...j'essaye de susciter --comme tous les hommes honnêtes de ma génération-- une in-

18José Corrales Egea, pp. 84-88.

quiétude politique.... J'adopte une attitude de dénon-
ciation et, naturellement, clairement engagée. (p. 4)

Juan García Hortelano: Affirmer, au moyen de mes
romans, que la société est susceptible de changement
et d'amélioration, voilà ce qui constitue mon plus in-
time devoir. (p. 7)

J. M. Caballero-Bonald: Il faut se jeter dans le
monde espagnol, contre vents et marées, et écrire
tout ce que l'on voit et entend, ce qui est déjà bien
suffisant. J'insiste sur le fait que cette reproduction
objective de la réalité est la seule formule valable pour
permettre à l'écrivain de remplir son rôle social. (p. 4)

A year after the interviews in *Les Lettres Français*, in October
of 1963 at a literary conference in Madrid, the Spanish delegation
of novelists sharply attacked the French new novelists for sup-
porting a *desengagé* novel. Conversely, the French condemned
the Spanish writers for their anachronistic --i.e., neorealistic, *engagé*-- attitude toward literature. But as José Corrales Egea
notes, the entire polemic was rather ironic, because the Spanish
realistic novel had nearly exhausted itself, while the French *nouveau roman* was being called by many critics the *vieux roman*,
"una fórmula vieja que producía tedio y lasitud."[19]

If by the early 1960's objective realism was no longer viewed
as the principal element for the future of the Spanish novel, then
two important questions must be answered: 1) why did the
movement away from realism occur? 2) what are the basic characteristics displayed by the new prose fiction, if indeed a new
novel is developing in Spain? The first question is somewhat easy
to answer, while the second will be answered in depth during the
remainder of our study of Juan Benet.

During the 1960's many of the social conditions and attitudes
prevalent in Spain during the previous two decades either ceased
to exist or grew steadily less important. Spanish isolation from
Europe and America slowly began to diminish. The massive
tourist industry in Spain bolstered the economy, and industrial-

---

[19]José Corrales Egea, p. 205.

14

ized growth increased substantially. The emigration and subsequent return of hundreds of thousands of Spanish workers also influenced the changing attitudes and social conditions in Spain. Returning immigrants brought with them new life styles and growing demands for change within their own culture. In addition, the gradual reduction of the strict censorship laws enabled both Hispanic and non-Hispanic works to be published in Spain for the first time, thereby facilitating American and European literary influence on both writers and the reading public. The generation of people born after 1935, for whom the Civil War is more of an historical fact than a lived reality, also have played an important role in the changing Spanish society. The war and its resultant social conditions of the 1940's and 1950's are of less interest to the young, contemporary reader because of his temporal separation from many of the post-war problems. Thus the Spanish novelist, who for twenty years had been utilizing the realistic novel as a social tool, in the 1960's begins to alter his purely social orientation and becomes more concerned with esthetics and experimentation. The novel of objective realism becomes, according to Corrales Egea, "desfasada": "...si al filo del medio siglo un puñado de jóvenes novelistas había sabido hacer la novela que las circunstancias exigían y justificaban, quince años después empezaban a estar desfasados con respecto a las nuevas circunstancias."[20]

The publication of Luis Martín Santos' *Tiempo de silencio* (1962) signifies what most critics agree is a crucial turning point in the evolution of the contemporary Spanish novel. Although Martín Santos' novel displays a marked social orientation --criticism not only of Madrid, but a pessimistic and destructive view of Spanish society as a whole--, it represents a significant departure from the objective realism which precedes it. *Tiempo de silencio* is a more complex and intellectual novel than those of the purely objective-realistic tendencies because Martín Santos experiments with language, style and technique. He clearly aspires to transcend the purely anecdotal aspect of his narrative in order to emphasize metaphysical, ideological and linguistic concerns.

[20]José Corrales Egea, p. 141.

Tiempo de silencio resembles Cela's *La colmena* in that it attempts to portray the social conditions of Madrid during a particular moment in history. However, the differences between the two novels in style, technique and point of view far outweigh any superficial similarities. Martín Santos bitterly criticizes a Spanish society which he believes is oppressed by a profound mental paralysis. Neither the poor nor the rich escape his disapproving eye. Yet it is not his critical attitude (e.g., he repeats many of Unamuno's ideas), but rather his manner of writing that is new. As Pablo Gil Casado notes, "La prosa de *Tiempo de silencio* es eminentemente barroca.... Hay, además, una considerable tendencia a lo experimental y desusado."[21] Frequently, Martín Santos creates neologisms, especially using medical terminology as a point of departure. He also employs unorthodox punctuation and often leaves proper names uncapitalized. His sentences are generally complex, with several clauses and enumerations which result in lengthy paragraphs. As Gil Casado has shown, Martín Santos possesses "una prosa vertiginosa, que podría llamarse 'automática,' por su parecido con cierta poesía del período surrealista."[22] Clearly, Martín Santos rejects a *casticista* view of the Spanish language, and throughout his novel displays an innovative attitude toward linguistic expression.

Tiempo de silencio is presented from various perspectives (interior and exterior), with an abundance of introspection, interior monologue, dialogue and third person narration. It is therefore in direct contrast to both the objective-realistic and behaviorist tendencies which precede it in Spain. Although his career as a writer was cut short by his premature death, Martín Santos brought to the art of novel writing in Spain an experimental attitude which had been nonexistent since the Civil War.

Although *Tiempo de silencio* represented an extraordinary protest against traditional realism, no unified movement against the realistic novel arose until the end of the 1960's. José Corrales Egea is more specific, claiming that from 1968 to 1970, "la protesta irrumpe de lleno y vigorosamente, tomando las proporcio-

---

[21]Pablo Gil Casado, pp. 286-287.
[22]Pablo Gil Casado, p. 289.

nes de un verdadero movimiento de rechazo, de una verdadera 'Contraola' antirrealista en todos los sentidos, lo mismo en cuanto a la construcción y a la forma de la obra narrativa, que en cuanto a los motivos incitadores y a la sustancia interna de la misma."[23] It must be noted, however, that the "contraola" of which Corrales Egea speaks does not necessarily refer to new novelists, but rather to new types of novels: *Señas de identidad* (1966) and *La reivindicación del conde don Julián* (1970) by Juan Goytisolo, Cela's *San Camilo, 1936* (1969), or *La parábola del náufrago* (1969) by Miguel Delibes.

Scant critical research has been undertaken on the group of writers which Corrales Egea calls the "contraola," primarily because their novels are still being written and no single, decisive tendency has emerged. Nevertheless, certain observations can be made concerning these writers. In the first place, the counter-wave writers aspire to make a *tabula rasa* of nearly all the works of the Generation of 1950. Using *Tiempo de silencio* as an affirmative point of departure, they have exhibited an ever-increasing interest in style, language and experimentation in form and narrative techniques.

One of the fundamental changes in the recent Spanish novel is a rejection of objective realism in favor of subjectivism. Initiated by *Tiempo de silencio*, the subjective influence is evident in such works as *Señas de identidad* and *Don Julián*, or Benet's Proustian *Una meditación* (1970). The latter novel best exemplifies the introspective, subjective world of the narrator-protagonist, and represents a complete antithesis to the behaviorist novel of the 1950's. By utilizing a first person narrator, interior monologue and retrospective memory, Benet achieves greater authenticity of a lived experience, and thereby overcomes more easily the mistrust of the reader concerning the veracity of fiction. As Antonio Vilanova notes concerning the movement toward subjectivism:

> En cuanto el novelista intenta describir los hechos
> sin revelar su presencia, adoptando un tono distante

---

[23]José Corrales Egea, p. 191.

e impersonal, como en la novela behaviorista, el lector no puede dejar de preguntarse quién está contando la historia. Por el contrario, cuando el protagonista se convierte en narrador de sus propias experiencias y recuerdos, en el analista de sus sentimientos y pasiones, en el intérprete del fluir de su conciencia y de sus estados de alma, el lector se ve forzado a admitir la visión de sí mismo que el personaje le ofrece desde dentro.[24]

The literary sources of the *contraola* writers are difficult to define precisely, but it can be asserted that these sources are not Spanish in origin. There is little doubt, for example, that the new novel of Latin America has had a considerable impact on Spanish writers. Mario Vargas Llosa, Carlos Fuentes and Guillermo Cabrera Infante all won important literary prizes in Spain during the 1960's, and have influenced both the Spanish writers and reading public. In addition, works by Faulkner, Hemingway, Proust, Joyce, Camus, Sartre, Woolf and others are becoming more easily obtainable by Spaniards, and have exercised great influence in Spain either directly in translation or indirectly through the novels of Latin American writers.

One of the most debated sources of influence on the recent Spanish novel is the French *nouveau roman*. The French new novel, cultivated and developed by such authors as Alain Robbe-Grillet, Claude Simon, Michel Butor, Nathalie Sarraute, Samuel Beckett and others, has undoubtedly affected the writing of contemporary Spanish novelists. Nevertheless, **the** question still remains whether the *nouveau roman* will be developed in Spain as an anachronism, similar to the novel of objective realism of the 1950's. José Corrales Egea suggests that it will. He claims that the writers of the Generation of 1950 did not recognize that the realistic novel was anachronistic during the period when they were writing it. Instead, only when the realistic novel began to decline in popularity did these novelists --and most critics-- begin to criticize it. Furthermore, the critical attitude toward ob-

---

[24]Antonio Vilanova, "De la objetividad al subjetivismo en la novela española actual," in *Prosa novelesca actual* (Universidad Internacional Menéndez Pelayo, 1967), pp. 135-136.

jective realism coincided with a growing awareness of literary developments outside of Spain. Hence, the *contraola* writers have appeared at the literary vanguard in Spain using as their principal model the *nouveau roman* which, as we have seen previously, is considered by many critics to be the *vieux roman*. As Corrales Egea points out, several elements of the literary theory of *contraola* writers are derived from the French new novel:

> A un realismo caduco, desprestigiado, se opone una vuelta a la subjetividad, al dominio de la subconciencia, a la imaginativa; al mismo tiempo que a una obligada preocupación social, a un compromiso de principio se opone un completo *desengagement* del escritor, una despolitización de su obra y una rehabilitación del arte por el arte. Contravalores, todos ellos, que el *nouveau roman* había adoptado desde hace tiempo y que volvemos a encontrar (como la imagen que devuelve el espejo), en los argumentos y teorías de los defensores de nuestra novela de los dos últimos años (1968-1970).25

In the broadest of terms, the French new novelists are united by several characteristics which recur in their works: a new approach to character portrayal and development, based primarily upon the rejection of traditional psychological elements; a disregard for chronology of events; prominence given to objects and space; an unorthodox treatment of dialogue; the substitution of pattern for plot; an intense concern for literary craftsmanship. Since these writers maintain a strictly *desengagé* attitude toward art, their only involvement is with writing itself. Referring to Robbe-Grillet in particular, M. García-Viñó offers perhaps the most succinct definition of the *nouveau roman*: "...el término *nouveau roman* no designa ni una escuela ni siquiera un grupo definido y constituido para un fin; es --o era, habría que decir-- una denominación cómoda para englobar a todos aquellos autores que buscan --o buscaban-- nuevas formas novelísticas, capaces de expresar nuevas relaciones entre el hombre y el mundo; a todos aquellos que están --o estaban--, en una palabra, de-

---

25José Corrales Egea, pp. 202-203.

cididos a reinventar la novela."[26] Clearly, the novels of Juan Benet, and the recent works of Cela, Delibes, Goytisolo and others
coincide with this definition.

It is evident that during the past decade objective realism has
ceased to exist as the essential characteristic of the Spanish novel. In contrast, experimentation and an attitude of "re-inven-
tion" of the novel have become dominant: "La mejor novelística
española de la década del 60 abandona su anterior sujeción al realismo y se enriquece con toda clase de experimentos formales y
expresivos, a tono con las corrientes predominantes de la novela
europea y americana, así del Norte como del Sur. Un espíritu
abierto a los nuevos modos de narrar, una concepción ágil y diná-
mica del arte de novelar, una mayor riqueza de puntos de vista y
formas de expresión, parecen prevalecer en los jóvenes narrado-
res de estos últimos años."[27]

One critic and author, Julián Ríos, has suggested that Juan
Benet and Juan Goytisolo are the most important Spanish novelists advancing this new and open spirit: "El nuevo Juan Goytisolo y Juan Benet; los dos protagonistas antagónicos de la nueva
novela española."[28] They are "antagónicos" because each offers a
different literary orientation for the future of the novel in Spain.
Whereas Goytisolo tends to fuse the experimental techniques of
the new novel of France and Latin America with an *engagé* attitude, Benet remains essentially *desengagé*, and reflects in his
novels various aspects of Faulkner, Proust and the new novel of
Latin America. Benet, of course, has only recently gained literary prominence, and a detailed analysis of his work has yet to be
done. Therefore, during the remainder of our present study we
shall examine the works of Juan Benet in order to discover the
major elements of both his novels and theory of literature, and
thereby define Benet's role as a "protagonista" in the development of the "nueva novela española."

[26]M. García-Viño, "Por una nueva novela," *Arbor*, 88 (1974), 133-137.

[27]Edenia Guillermo and Juana Amelia Hernández, *La novelística española de los sesenta* (New York: Eliseo Torres & Sons, 1971), p. 24.

[28]Julián Ríos, Pere Gimferrer and José María Castellet, "Encuesta: nueva literatura española," *Plural*, N° 25 (octubre de 1973), 4-7.

THE LITERARY THEORY OF JUAN BENET

Although Juan Benet is primarily an author of prose fiction, he has also written several essays on literary theory. *La inspiración y el estilo* (1966), Benet's most comprehensive study of the literary process, is a mélange of literary history, literary theory and practical criticism. However, it consists of a cohesive series of essays bound together by the recurrent treatment of style. In *Puerta de tierra* (1969), a collection of essays on a variety of topics, Benet offers a detailed analysis of metaphor and the associated problems of creativity and language usage. Other writings in *Puerta de tierra* vary in content from reflections on marriage in "Epístola moral a Laura," to a phenomenological study of the music of Franz Schubert in "Op Potsh." In all of his essays, and especially those which treat literary problems, Benet alludes to a wide variety of representative authors: Dante, Shakespeare, Matthew Arnold, Proust, Ercilla, Flaubert, Cervantes and several others. Indeed, Benet's essays illustrate not only that he is a well-informed literary intellectual, but that he also possesses a profound understanding of literature from the genesis of the creative process, to expression through language, to the role of critical reading and analysis. In each of these areas of the literary process, Benet writes with a profound insight which makes his essays on criticism rank in significance and novelty with his more widely known works of prose fiction.

In the "Prólogo" to the second edition of *La inspiración y el estilo*, Benet writes that, "en este libro traté de indagar la razón por la cual desapareció del castellano el *grand style* para dar paso al costumbrismo."[1] Although the historical development of the "grand style" forms an integral part of Benet's study, it constitutes only a minor element of the larger and more important problem of style in general. The title of the book suggests the

---

[1]Juan Benet, "Prólogo" to *La inspiración y el estilo*, 2nd ed. (Barcelona: Seix Barral, 1973), p. 20. Future references to *La inspiración y el estilo* will be from the first edition (Madrid: Revista de Occidente, 1966), and noted within parentheses in the text by page number and the letters "IE."

primary areas of Benet's attention --*inspiración*, *estilo*--, and it is on these two problems that the present chapter will concentrate. A third element, the metaphor, is another significant factor in Benet's overall view of literature. Treated in *La inspiración* in a cursory fashion, metaphor is given detailed analysis in "Epica, noética, poiética" of *Puerta de tierra*.

Benet also discusses other elements of the literary process in addition to those mentioned above. Many are correlative problems, such as language, creativity and imagination. Benet also emphasizes, as he states in the prologue of *La inspiración*, the historical changes which lead to the growth of the *costumbrista* movement and the fall of the "grand style" in Spain. This is especially evident in the chapters "La ofensiva de 1850" and "La entrada en la taberna." Nonetheless, these chapters, and the matters of discussion within them, are only supportive of the central themes which recur throughout Benet's essays. Therefore, for purposes of classification and more exact treatment, I have reduced my discussion of Benet's theory to three areas: style, inspiration and metaphor. Neither of the three terms can be excluded from the discussion of the others, but a study of each will provide an understanding of the whole of Benet's literary theory of *La inspiración y el estilo* and *Puerta de tierra*.

Style and Inspiration

Although the definition of style varies greatly among critics, there is almost unanimous agreement that style is always present in a work of art. As Susan Sontag points out, "there is no neutral, absolutely transparent style."[2] Even Camus' famous "white style" of *The Stranger* --impersonal, lucid, flat-- is itself the expression of Meursalt's image of the world. And what Roland Barthes has called "writing zero degree" is, by its dehumanized and antimetaphorical nature, as selective and personal as any more traditional style of writing.[3] Nevertheless, while

---

[2]Susan Sontag, "On Style," in *Against Interpretation*, 3rd printing (New York: Dell, 1970), p. 25.

[3]Sontag, "On Style," p. 25.

style is implicit in every literary work, an accepted definition and complete understanding of the complexities of style have yet to be delineated.

In *La inspiración y el estilo* Benet is well aware of the elusive qualities of style which seem to defy definition. He notes that it has never been possible to discuss style with either precision or vague generalities. The result has been that "se ha hecho con él [estilo] lo que se ha hecho con el hombre: definirlo lo menos posible y caracterizarlo hasta la saciedad" (p. 137, *IE*). Benet's own theories, of course, are not intended to serve as a panacea for the complicated problems implicit in the term, "style." Nevertheless, Benet's discussion includes a comprehensive analysis of style as it relates to imagination and inspiration, to expression through language and to the critical eye of the reader in terms of participation and comprehension. Benet does not define style, but he conveys through analysis and example what might be called an "understanding" of the term and its role in the literary process.

Benet first discusses style and inspiration in chapter one of *La inspiración y el estilo*. He claims that a writer can be inspired only when he possesses a style: "Yo no creo que la luz de la inspiración sea capaz de descubrir ningún hueco, porque la inspiración le es dada a un escritor sólo cuando posee un estilo o cuando hace suyo un estilo previo" (pp. 15-16, *IE*). Benet thus poses his central hypothesis that a cause and effect relationship exists between style and inspiration, but at this early stage of his essay we are unable to define precisely how this relation originates and functions.

The enigmas of inspiration have preoccupied poets and philosophers since early antiquity. For Socrates inspiration was a result of *theia moira*, or divine dispensation. According to this theory, the poet is unable to create until he has received the power to do so from the gods. If the gods regard him with disfavor, the poet is completely helpless to write at all. Although he disagrees with Socrates' theory, Benet elaborates upon it in *La inspiración*. He maintains that implicit in the power received from the gods is a transcendency of one's own condition through the process of "endiosamiento" (p. 24, *IE*). Once he is inspired the poet can participate in divine creation and, consequently, has a more direct communication with the universe than the normal man. Thus the poet's *estado de gracia* --Benet's term for the poet who has been inspired-- elevates him to the lofty position of contact with creation.[4]

Socrates' concept of inspiration underwent several minor changes through the centuries, but its essential elements remained stable. In later antiquity, for example, Longinus' treatise *On the Sublime* centered the idea of inspiration less on a divine source than in the thoughts and emotions of the poet's soul. Later, Plotinus integrates divine illumination into a more comprehensive philosophy of "divine intelligence and life radiant through and immanent in all the universe and all human souls and minds."[5] A specific instance of such intelligence is the poet or artist who, by some superior access to divinity, provides a better and brighter image of Zeus.

The theories of Longinus and Plotinus continued to stimulate discussion for several centuries. Even during the Romantic period of the eighteenth and nineteenth centuries, a vital and constant relationship was perceived to exist between the writer and a divine source.[6] But the Romantics altered the idea of inspiration by shifting from a theological-oriented to a more intimate and psychological theory of inspiration. In Benet's opinion, this more personal view of inspiration has remained popular into our own era, and is utilized by those who seek a magical answer to the mysteries of the creative process.

Although Benet understands the "divine dispensation" theory of inspiration, he finds it incomplete and unacceptable:

---

[4]Benet's assertion that the inspired poet participates (according to Socrates' theory) in divine creation clearly echoes S. T. Coleridge's theory of primary imagination: "The Imagination then, I consider either as primary, or secondary. The primary Imagination I hold to be the living power and prime Agent of all human perception, and as a repetition in the finite mind of the eternal act of creation in the infinite I am." "Biographia Literaria," in *The Complete Works of S. T. Coleridge* (New York: Harper and Brothers, 1868), p. 363.

[5]Charles Wimsatt and Cleanth Brooks, *Literary Criticism* (New York: Random House, 1957), p. 725.

[6]See especially S. T. Coleridge, as previously cited, and William Wordsworth in *Wordsworth's Literary Criticism*, ed. Nowell C. Smith (London, 1925).

> Yo adelanto ya mi proposición: el estilo proporciona el estado de gracia; a mi modo de ver, y a falta de otro término más específico, es preciso buscar en el estilo esa región del espíritu que, tras haber desahuciado a los dioses que la habitaban, se ve en la necesidad de subrogar sus funciones para proporcionar al escritor una vía evidente de conocimiento, independiente y casi trascendente a ciertas funciones del intelecto, que le faculte para una descripción cabal del mundo y que, en definitiva, sea capaz de suministrar cualquier género de respuesta a las preguntas que en otra ocasión el escritor elevaba a la divinidad. (p. 26, *IE*)

Benet eschews the idea of divine illumination and claims that style provides the *estado de gracia* from which the poet obtains a transcendental knowledge --independent of normal, intellectual knowledge-- of the world which he must portray in his writing.

"Literature and Reason"

Benet's discussion of transcendental knowledge of the world, as distinct from an intellectual or cognitive view of reality, forms a fundamental aspect of the relation between style and inspiration in the work of art. Early in his career, Benet believed that inspiration involved an act of knowledge which was closely related to reason (*razón*) and the writer's will (*voluntad*). That is, the writer, with the aid of his deductive faculties, could carry out a particular literary project determined by his will. In *La inspiración y el estilo*, however, Benet maintains a firm anti-rationalist attitude toward writing because he believes that reason (and *a posteriori* intellectual knowledge) inhibits the flow of the creative process. He claims that reason is merely a specific and brief moment of inspiration, and not the main axis on which inspiration turns. If the writer is to create anything, he must transcend the barriers imposed by reason in order to gain a deeper insight into the enigmas of reality and unreality. Benet strongly suggests that the author's style is the tool which must be utilized both to explore and express these mysteries.

The will (an instrument of reason), however, maintains a significant role in Benet's theory because it creates a tension between the desire to undertake a literary project and the need for expression. The result of this tension is the creation of inspiration. But since the need for expression is paramount --otherwise there is no work of art-- it is style that must be used to achieve this goal. Thus style becomes both the source and vehicle of expression of inspiration.

In order to illustrate further his view of reason and logic in the creative process, Benet undertakes a detailed study of Edgar Allan Poe's *The Philosophy of Composition*. Poe envisages the poet as a craftsman who brings his intelligence and knowledge to bear fully on the problem of organizing words into specific literary structures. He maintains that the writing of a poem should not be a matter of accident or intuition, but rather should reveal "the precision and rigid consequence of a mathematical problem."[7] Poe implies that during the creative process of a writer --or at least during the creative process of an *imaginative* writer-- a chronological series of functions takes place: 1) inspiration; 2) imagination; 3) analysis of the result of imagination. The latter process is mandatory because it unveils the secrets of the first two. Thus Poe suggests that the ultimate value of a literary work is not the enigmas within it, but rather that the work has value only insofar as its meaning can be shown by rigorous, mathematical reasoning.

Benet objects to Poe's theory for two reasons: 1) it emphasizes reason and logic as the nucleus of writing; 2) it suggests that the ultimate value of the literary work for the reader is linked directly to the process of creation. But as Benet points out, it is one thing to write a poem in agreement with a logical outline, and quite another for the reader to analyze and untangle it using the same scheme. (p. 57, *IE*).

What in essence Benet objects to about Poe's rational approach to both the writing of a poem and the reader's subsequent discovery of its meaning, parallels Eliseo Vivas' well-known ob-

---

[7]Edgar Allan Poe, "The Philosophy of Composition," in *Works* (New York & London: Funk and Wagnalls, 1904), Vol. I, p. 6.

jection to T. S. Eliot's "objective correlative." Both Benet and Vivas accept the work of art as an object in the hands of the reader, but object to the idea of the work serving as a vehicle for transferal of emotion between writer and reader. The poet only discovers his emotion by formulating it in words, not by means of a preconceived plan. Consequently, it is impossible for the reader to feel the same emotion as the poet did and, as Vivas points out, there is no reason why he should.[8] Benet, however, would expand Vivas' theory to include a rejection of any rational or logical plan capable of formulating, or subsequently revealing the meaning of a literary work, particularly when referring to the author's style.

During a certain moment of the literary process the writer must describe and translate into words the ideas and images of his mind. Benet claims that at some point during this process of expression the writer will extend his mind to an unknown zone which his reason cannot clearly define. The ideas and images of this enigmatic reality do not correspond to words he finds in the dictionary, nor can they be expressed by normal forms of language. The writer must therefore invent a pellicle (*película*) capable of receiving the impressions of images which lie outside the realm of rational thought. This pellicle is the writer's style, which is carefully developed over a long period of time in order to transcend intellectual knowledge and therefore express the obscure images and hidden concepts of the writer's mind. (pp. 141-142, *IE*) Conversely, a writer who restricts himself to only those areas where reason exercises its power, is an incomplete and less desirable writer because he has not fully developed a style. For this reason Benet rejects the literary value of the nineteenth-century *costumbrista* and Naturalist authors.

The ability to express enigmatic images and ideas traditionally has been associated with inspiration. That is, the writer receives divine dispensation and is favored with a certain *estado de gracia* which enables him to rise above the common man. However, as we have seen, Benet rejects this theory and asserts his

---

[8]Eliseo Vivas, "The Objective Correlative of T. S. Eliot," in *Creation and Discovery* (New York: Noonday Press, 1955).

own belief that inspiration is possible only when it is directly related to an author's carefully developed style: "De forma que... sólo le es dable esperarla [inspiración] a quien se ha ocupado de organizar una estructura que le ayude a la comprensión total, la trascendencia y... la invención de la realidad" (p. 147, *IE*). It is not the writer's reason which enables him to transcend and invent reality, but rather his style, his peculiar use of images, metaphors or certain preferred words and phrases. Thus Benet can affirm that "el escritor se encara con el mundo que le rodea menos mediante una ciencia cognoscitiva que gracias a una estilística, que es la que le dicta la imagen general del universo..." (p. 92, *IE*).

For Benet, therefore, writing which is based solely on reason is antithetical to inspiration. Inspiration is linked directly to the author's style, which in turn is developed only when rational thought is abandoned. Style reifies inspiration and enables the author to invent new realities. The writer thus participates in a type of divine creation, but according to Benet, he receives no divine illumination.

"Form and Content"

Benet's preoccupation with style provides the impetus for an in-depth study of the traditional distinction between form and content in a literary work. Benet analyzes the problem from an extrinsic and historical point of view, using the nineteenth-century novel as a point of departure, as well as from an intrinsic point of view. He accepts the distinction between content and form as a necessary one, but also suggests a more subtle separation of *estilo* and *información*.

Benet categorizes the Realistic and Naturalistic novel of the second half of the nineteenth century as "una novela documental," which is totally deficient in literary value. He maintains that the authors of this period were overwhelmed by scientific advances and social evolution, and were concerned in their novels with the "informational" aspect of writing: i.e., content. (p. 117, *IE*) All other literary elements were subordinated to the objective representation of contemporary society, with the result

being an ephemeral literature which today has little or no interest
for the reader. There were, however, certain novels written during this period which have survived temporal interests and are
read today. *Moby Dick*, for example, continues to arouse our
interest, not because it is about whaling, but because of the form
which Melville gave the narrative and the particular manner of
expression. That is, because of Melville's style.

In *For a New Novel*, Alain Robbe-Grillet asserts that "...the
genuine writer has nothing to say. He has only a way of speaking."[9] Thus for Robbe-Grillet the value of literary art lies in the
author's style. Benet clearly echoes Robbe-Grillet's view of style.
While dismissing the nineteenth-century documentary novel as
lacking literary value, Benet affirms his own commitment to the
importance of style: "Y aquí rozamos uno de los grandes temas
del problema del estilo: el que la cosa literaria sólo puede tener
·interés por el estilo, nunca por el asunto" (p. 118, *IE*). Literature
does not exist *a priori* as a valid means of portraying society
(which the Naturalists believed), but rather becomes literature
and acquires literary value only when the author is concerned
with the *manner* in which he expresses himself.

Benet's distinction between style and information (*estilo* and
información) is not the traditional separation of form and content. Whereas the latter combination always remains distinct
from each other, style and information must necessarily coincide. Benet defines content as everything that is discussed or
portrayed in a novel, while information is more specific: "No se
puede llamar información a todo lo que dice el escritor, sino a
aquello que dice con cierto propósito de docencia, aprovechando
el desnivel entre sus conocimientos y la ignorancia del lector" (p.
122, *IE*). By *docencia*, Benet does not imply a moral purpose,
but simply the information which the writer provides the reader
concerning their surrounding reality.

The distinction which Benet makes between form and style is
even more important. Form refers only to the structure of a sentence, the use of certain words and the harmony of meaning.

[9]Alain Robbe-Grillet, *For a New Novel*, trans. Richard Howard, 2nd ed. (New
York: Grove Press, 1965), p. 45.

Style, however, encompasses much more, "porque toma sobre sí no sólo todas las modalidades de dicción, sino el interés de toda la información. Dentro de ese complicado organismo el estilo asume todas las funciones dinámicas y se configura como un sistema que aprovecha el desnivel originado por la información para crear un movimiento de interés, que mantiene su marcha incluso por inercia, cuando aquel desnivel se anula" (p. 122, *IE*). Style, therefore, provides a means of overcoming the ephemeral quality of a literary work. A nineteenth-century novel, for example, may have been of interest to the nineteenth-century reader because of its "informational" elements. But as Benet points out, the informative nature of the novel maintains its interest only as long as readers recognize it as part of their reality. In contrast, the style of a novel can overcome the purely extrinsic interest of the content and give the work a timeless quality.

Susan Sontag, in her essay "On Style," concurs with the assertion that style is the most significant aspect of art. In fact, she claims that "style is art." But whereas Benet makes the traditional distinction between content and form (and emphasizes the latter), Sontag argues convincingly that the distinction should be abolished. She maintains that, "A work of art encountered as a work of art is an experience... and the knowledge we gain through art is an experience of the form or style of knowing something rather than a knowledge of something (like a fact or a moral judgement) in itself."[10] However, Benet's recognition of a separation between the content and form of a literary work is a necessary one for his theory of the nineteenth-century novel. As we have seen, Benet believes that during the second half of the nineteenth century writers were overwhelmed by the new discoveries of science and the theories of social evolution. The description of man and his social environment became the principal *raison d'être* of the novel. As a result, the informational aspect of literature subordinated all other elements. Since Benet criticizes this documentary or informational writing he must necessarily distinguish between content and the form which it takes. While asserting the predominance of style, Benet is unable to eliminate the concept of content, because by doing so he would destroy his

10Susan Sontag, "On Style," p. 30.

own theory on the failure of nineteenth-century prose fiction.

"History and Poetry"

In "La seriedad del estilo," the final chapter of *La inspiración y el estilo*, Benet discusses Aristotle's famous distinction between history and poetry. According to the Greek philosopher, while both forms of writing tell us *about* something, poetry is more truthful and more serious. For several hundred years scholars have debated and attempted to explain this statement, and according to Benet, have in general either distorted or totally misunderstood Aristotle's intentions.

Benet believes that Aristotle was probably referring to Homer when he made the distinction between poetry and history. Homer was able to narrate "una historia," but at the same time he succeeded in transcending "la simple verosimilitud, exactitud, realidad e interés de unos hechos que fueron" (p. 146, *IE*). Benet insists that the difference between poetry and history does not pertain to the subject matter, but rather to the intentions of the author: "Historiadores y poetas cuentan las mismas cosas, con distinta dicción, para alcanzar objetivos distintos" (p. 146, *IE*). In the final analysis, it is the impression which the author desires to leave on the subject matter that distinguishes the poet and historian.

The impression created by the author, according to Benet, is a direct result of style. Whereas the historian is interested in the particular nature of the facts, the poet is more concerned with "la segunda realidad" (p. 148, *IE*), which he invents with his style. Benet thus reaffirms here the recurring theme of his book: not only through style can the writer transcend the limits of his surrounding reality, but he is also capable of inventing reality. Both the historian and the poet relate *some thing*, but the latter also invents. In this light we can now understand why Benet entitles his chapter, "La seriedad del estilo." If, as Aristotle insists, poetry is serious, and if we accept Benet's view that style is the most important aspect of poetry, it follows that style must also be serious. But as we have seen, style is not only serious, it is the essential element of any literary work.

32

Metaphor

Benet's preoccupation with metaphor can be viewed as a direct consequence of his interest in style and expression. In *La inspiración y el estilo*, Benet discusses the importance of metaphor only briefly, and entirely within an historical context. In his essay, "Epica, noética, poiética,"[11] however, he provides a detailed analysis of the creative qualities of metaphoric expression, and offers a unique explanation of the origin of the metaphor.

Benet claims that the origin of the metaphor is intimately related to the epic poems of antiquity. The epic poet narrates a diversified series of events about gods and super humans that have never actually occurred, and therefore have never been witnessed. However, the deeds which are portrayed in epic poetry are related directly to human experience, because everthing that the poet narrates *can* be experienced or witnessed by men, only on a much smaller scale. The epic hero is therefore similar to the common man in terms of potential experiences, and distinguished only by exaggerated circumstances. (pp. 19-20, *PT*)

The essential problem which the epic poet confronts, then, is how to define a series of events which the reader (or listener) has never seen. It is not a matter of simply magnifying the events to a "bigger-than-life" appearance, but rather involves the delineation of an exact scale of proportions between two sets of images --the human and super-human-- which permits one element to form a homologous relationship with the other through a simple process of conversion. And it is precisely within this method of conversion, believes Benet, that the origin of the metaphor can be found:

> Yo tengo para mí... que la tan debida cuestión del origen de la metáfora radica ahí, en la perentoria necesidad que siente el poeta de suministrar al lector... la escala de referencia entre lo que aquél describe y lo que éste conoce por experiencia. Y así como en la co-

---

[11]Juan Benet, "Epica, noética, poiética," in *Puerta de tierra* (Barcelona: Seix Barral, 1970). All references to *Puerta de tierra* will be from this edition and noted within parentheses in the text by page number and the letters "PT."

> lección de planos que define una obra se inscribe en
> cada uno de ellos esa escala o relación entre las mag-
> nitudes de la obra dibujada y la obra que debe ser re-
> alizada, así en cada una de las páginas de la epopeya
> se debe insertar la correspondiente metáfora que re-
> cuerda al lector la proporción que existe entre los he-
> chos épicos y los hechos humanos a que está acostum-
> brado. (pp. 22-23, *PT*)

The above type of metaphor, which Benet calls a "scaling metaphor," first appeared in the epic poetry of Homer, and has become the characteristic feature of all epic poetry which has attempted to compare the fabulous and the human. However, as
Benet points out, there are countless relationships between
things and ideas which transcend the expressive power of the
scaling metaphor. In order to express more abstract and ethereal
concepts, the poet must utilize what Benet calls a "modal metaphor": "Metáfora no escalar --no se trata de dar la representación
de una dimensión-- sino modal, definitoria de un gesto, de una
actitud..." (p. 26, *PT*).

Although Benet's distinction between "modal" and "scaling"
metaphors is based on historical study of epic poetry, the true
value of his discussion lies outside of historical considerations.
His primary concern is with literary invention and expression.
The themes of literature, of course, may be repeated: "La literatura... se enfrenta, antes que con otra cosa, con el tema del hombre en la naturaleza y resulta forzoso que se repita, que incida
una y otra vez sobre los mismos temas inmediatos que han sido
tratados por los viejos autores" (p. 39, *PT*). Innovation must
therefore be viewed in terms of style and the writer's personal
manner of expression. Thus implicit in Benet's analysis of metaphor is the fundamental theme of all of his literary theory: in
Marshall McLuhan's terminology, "the medium is the mes-
sage." Benet is not concerned with the fact that epic poets wrote
of gods and super humans. Rather, he is interested in their use of
language to express --or invent-- both the apparent and enigmatic elements of reality.

Benet's theory of how the metaphor functions resembles in
many respects José Ortega y Gasset's concept of the metaphor.
Early in his career Ortega devoted several essays to the origin

and function of the metaphor,[12] and at least a few of his ideas play a major role in Benet's theory. According to Ortega, the metaphor may be of use to both the scientist and the poet. For example, when a scientific investigator discovers a new phenomenon (or a new concept), he needs to give it a name. Since a new word would have meaning to no one but the discoverer, it becomes necessary to utilize already existing language, where words have an *a priori*, designated meaning. In order to make himself understood, the scientist selects a word whose "accepted" meaning has some similarity with the new meaning it is to acquire. In this way the word gains new expression through the process of transposition, and does not entirely abandon its original signification. Ortega warns, however, that although metaphor actually means "transposition," not all such processes form metaphors: those transpositions in which "una voz pasa de tener un sentido a tener otro, pero con abandono del primero" (Vol. II, p. 389).

Ortega's definition of metaphor closely resembles one given by W. B. Stanford in his book *Greek Metaphor*. Like Ortega, Stanford stresses the semantic aspect of metaphor, and offers the following definition:

> The term metaphor is fully valid only when applied to a very definite and a rather complicated concept, *viz.* the process and result of using a term (X) normally signifying an object or concept (A) in such a context that it must refer to another object or concept (B), which is distinct enough in characteristics from A to ensure that in the composite idea formed by the synthesis of the concepts A and B and now symbolized in the word X, the factors A and B retain their conceptual independence even while they merge in the unity symbolized by X...[13]

For both Ortega and Stanford metaphor "means" a third thing,

---

[12]Among the most important of Ortega's essays on metaphor are "Las dos grandes metáforas," "La teología de Renán," and "Las tres grandes metáforas." See *Obras completas* (Madrid: Revista de Occidente, 1963), Vol. III.

[13]W. B. Stanford, *Greek Metaphor* (Oxford: B. Blackwell, 1963), p. 105.

different from the meaning of either of its terms viewed in isolation.

Although Benet does not offer a theory concerning the semantic independence of the original elements of the metaphor, he does emphasize the transposition ("conversion" in Benet's terminology) of both Ortega and Stanford. More important, however, is the similarity between Ortega and Benet's proposition that metaphor aids in the invention of reality. Ortega claims that not only does the metaphor assist in naming something difficult to name, but it also aids our conceptualization of the "thing" itself. The metaphor, therefore, is a knowledge of realities. But as Julián Marías points out, Ortega's theory of metaphor also implies that in one of its dimensions poetry is investigation, and discovers or invents realities in a similar manner to scientific exploration.[14] And as we have seen, Benet concurs with Ortega that the metaphor, as an important element of style, is capable of inventing or discovering the enigmas of reality.

"Metaphor and Hyperbole"

Similar to I. A. Richards, Benet views the metaphor in part as a comparing process, and he patterns his terminology of the metaphorical components after Richards' concept of *tenor* and *vehicle*.[15] Originally, the metaphor was used to transform through analogy a literary object to an object of identifiable reality: "De acuerdo con esta función de los dos términos de la comparación, el primero --el comparable-- es siempre un objeto de la fábula; el segundo --el comparado-- de la realidad" (p. 29, *PT*). Frequently, however, a process of inversion of these two elements occurs which totally changes the character and function of the metaphor. This process, the result of which Benet calls hyperbole, consists of taking the "comparable" element from reality and the "compared" element from a literary source.

[14]Julián Marías, *Ortega: Circunstancia y vocación* (Madrid: Revista de Occidente, 1960), p. 294.

[15]I. A. Richards. *The Philosophy of Rhetoric* (New York & London: Oxford University Press, 1936). See specifically chapters V and VI.

Although hyperbole occurred in the earliest epic poems, Benet believes it is primarily a result of an intellectual, esoteric atmosphere of writing. Such was the case, for example, during the *cultista* period of sixteenth- and seventeenth-century Spain. For the writers of this time it became customary to avoid making references to objects from reality without first leading the reader peripatetically through a second, literary reality made up of inverted metaphors. It is during this period, believes Benet, that the function of the metaphor becomes ambiguous and contradictory, and hyperbole reaches its apogee. (p. 30, *PT*)

Yet there exists, as Benet belatedly points out, a logical explanation for the *cultista* development of hyperbole. When the poet's frame of reference is limited to artistic and literary events, then this world becomes as "real" and as common as quotidian, observable reality. Consequently, the poet may forget that, while certain things and experiences are common to him and his peers, they are quite unusual for the large majority of the people. That is, the frame of reference on which metaphors are based becomes restrictive. When both elements of the metaphor (the *comparable* and *comparado*) are constructed using fictitious or unreal elements, the process of inversion itself becomes exaggerated and hyperbole is the result.

"Epic and Lyric"

Benet adds a new dimension to his study of metaphor by making an unusual distinction between the epic and lyric poet. The writer of epic poetry, believes Benet, attempts to portray things he has never seen or directly experienced before. In contrast, the lyric poet can avoid this problem because the things he writes about (love, solitude, melancholy, etc.), and the devices which he uses in his poetry (roses, sunsets, etc.) form part of almost everyone's frame of reference. Consequently, he does not need to describe them. Whereas the epic poet relates the "nunca visto," the lyric writer tells of "lo común," of what is contained in the mind of all people. Nevertheless, both poets are united by a common purpose: "...narrar una cosa única que, sea ordinaria o extraordinaria, se aparte de las demás y cuente con los suficientes valores individuales como para ocupar por derecho propio un puesto en el mundo del arte" (pp. 42-43, *PT*).

While the two poets share the goal of "narrar una cosa única," they employ different methods of writing. The epic poet transforms the extraordinary into something intelligible, almost ordinary. The lyric poet, on the other hand, attempts to make something extraordinary out of the most common events or ideas and, as a result, often creates hyperbole. The transformation achieved by the epic poet (extraordinary > ordinary) leads Benet to his principal conclusion concerning the origin and function of the metaphor: "Yo creo que es el épico quien inventa la metáfora para dar solución a todo el ciclo que implica su propósito: 1) inventar algo muy singular que el hombre no ha visto ni soñado; 2) hacerlo inteligible gracias a la escala de conversión de lo sobrenatural a lo natural, de lo singular a lo común. Para recorrer el mismo camino pero en sentido inverso el lírico lo único que tiene que hacer es darle la vuelta a la metáfora, comparando lo común a lo extraordinario o lo que es lo mismo, haciendo hipérboles" (p. 43, *PT*).[16]

As we have seen previously in *La inspiración y el estilo*, the middle of the 1800's marked a significant change in the development of prose fiction. It signified, according to Benet, "la entrada en la taberna" --the *Costumbrista* and Naturalistic period of writing. But the fifty-year period prior to 1850 was perhaps even more significant, because the novel underwent a complete metamorphic cycle. This cycle began with Romanticism, during which time the point of departure and primary interest of the writer was the story he was going to tell. But by mid-century Flaubert's developing prose represents a complete transformation of this concept. The writer's principal interest becomes the "means" of expression. The formulation of a perfect prose becomes the ultimate goal of the writer, who is now concerned purely with style. (pp. 64-65, *IE*)

Although the cycle was complete in 1850 with Flaubert, Benet

---

[16]Benet also relates the philosopher to the epic poet. After establishing that the epic poet tells of things that have never been seen before, Benet concludes that, "El pensador es también un épico en medida que nadie ha visto ni oído aquello acerca de lo que va a hablar" (p. 43, *PT*).

claims that the change in emphasis from content to style is a direct result of the evolution of the metaphor during a period of approximately fifty years. During this time the metaphoric function gradually grows nebulous because the metaphor no longer represents "some thing." The two component parts of the metaphor fuse into a single entity, which itself is no longer a symbol, but rather a thing in itself. Flaubert, the great stylist, develops the metaphor as a "thing" or an "object," until it becomes the principal element of his writing. For Flaubert, then, style relegates all other elements of writing to minor functions, a concept which Benet insists is the essence of all literature.

Although the essays in *La inspiración y el estilo* and "Epica, noética, poiética" of *Puerta de tierra* use literary history as a point of departure, the problems which Benet discusses transcend temporal concerns and emphasize matters common to literature of all epochs. Every writer must confront the literary process from creativity to expression through his chosen medium of language. As we have seen, Benet insists that the ultimate value of a literary work coincides with the particular way in which the author comes to terms with language. That is, the value of literature *qua* literature depends upon the writer's style --all that is implicit in a writer's personal, intimate use of language which is capable of inventing realities and transcending the interest of content.

Benet's theory of the relationship between style and inspiration, however, remains somewhat ambiguous. In contrast to the traditional "divine dispensation" theory of inspiration, Benet maintains that inspiration is inextricably bound to style, and therefore, to language. Thus style (language) becomes both the source and mode of expression of inspiration. Of course, Benet's theory cannot be proved or disproved in an experimental, scientific sense. But what we can and must demand from any literary theory is consistency and articulate expression. Whereas Benet remains constant in his basic assumption concerning the primacy of style in the literary work, his own circumventive style guides us peripatetically through literary history and theory which frequently remains abstract and confused. Can the writer who does not possess a well developed style be inspired? Benet answers that he cannot. But perhaps what Benet intends is that the inspired writer who has no style is only incapable of giving linguistic expression to inspiration. In either case, it is an unresolved problem with a direct parallel to the eternal puzzle of "the chicken and the egg."

If style is the essence of literature, then the metaphor constitutes the most important element of style. Benet agrees with Ortega that metaphor is a means of expression and mode of discovery: it is both a process of naming and inventing. However, can the writer really invent anything? If we view language as the set of all grammatically acceptable combinations of words, then the metaphor is merely a juxtaposition of words which are not normally associated with each other. Is the poet in fact "creating" realities in the strictest meaning of the word? Or is he instead fulfilling the role of what we might call a "facilitator?" That is, as a result of some special ability (which Benet would consider to be a combination of style and inspiration), the poet manipulates language to *suggest* new literary realities by utilizing the *a priori*, designated "meaning" of words. But how can the reader identify these "new realities" if he does not share the author's frame of reference upon which invention and metaphor are based?

Benet stresses the concept of a shared frame of reference between writer and reader in order for communication to take place. He implicitly rejects Eliot's "objective correlative" and claims that at the minimum inter-subjective viability is required for poetic communication. As W. K. Wimsatt has written concerning this problem: "It will not be enough for a reader to be instructed (by a theorist or by a historian) that once upon a time, here and there, this meant that, purple was royal, black meant death, Dorian was martial, Lydian erotic, flutes were sweet, thunder frightening. If a poem is actually experienced and valued, these things no less than (and as a condition for) the deeper poetic meanings of spirit, must lie somehow within the range of experience."[17]

Benet's view of metaphor and experience seems to echo what Coleridge affirmed about language in general: "Be it observed...

[17]Wimsatt and Brooks, p. 739.

that I include in the *meaning* of a word not only its correspon-
dent object, but likewise all the associations which it recalls. For
language is framed to convey not the object alone, but likewise
the character, mood and intentions of the person who is repre-
senting it."[18] But the reader's experience must not be such that
a process of distortion occurs. The reader must react to the metaphor (and language in general) in a manner which maintains the
inner coherence of the literary work. While affirming that words
have an "accepted meaning," as well as a more personal, "experienced" meaning for the reader, Benet would agree with I. A.
Richards that words also possess a context meaning as they
"interanimate" with one another.[19] Words are qualified by the
entire context in which they are placed, and thus bring to that
context powers derived from other contexts in which they have
figured in the past. Thus metaphoric expression demands both
intrinsic and extrinsic response from the reader.

Benet could have resolved many of the ambiguities of style
and expression in his theory had he approached language as
being problematic. However, he does not treat the problem of
language and its role in the process from thought (or pre-
thought) to expression in written words. He assumes that language is a faithful reflection of the author's intention, and thereby avoids the difficult task of dealing with the precise nature of
literary creation. In this respect we might classify Benet's view
of language as "classical," at least in Jorge Luis Borges' concept
of classicism. Borges claims that "classical" does not describe
writers of a particular historical period, but rather refers to the
writer who has confidence in the power of accepted language to
say anything he desires to say: "Distraigo aquí de toda connota-
ción histórica las palabras *clásico* y *romántico*; entiendo por ellas
dos arquetipos de escritor (dos procederes). El clásico no descon-
fía del lenguaje, cree en la suficiente virtud de cada uno de sus
signos."[20] Benet, however, would deny any theoretical identifi-

[18]S. T. Coleridge, *Biographia Literaria*, p. 485.

[19]Richards' "context theory" of meaning is developed in two books: *The Meaning of Meaning* (1923) and *The Philosophy of Rhetoric* (1936).

[20]Jorge Luis Borges, "La postulación de la realidad," in *Discusión*, 5th ed.
(Buenos Aires: Emecé, 1969), p. 67.

cation with classical attitudes because he believes that the classical periods of history restricted the expressive faculties of the writer. It would appear, then, that Benet views literary creation primarily as the manipulation of language (and specifically the metaphor). But the precise nature and processes of the creative act are unclear, except that style is the motivating and substantive element.

Juan Benet's theory of literature is not modeled after any one particular school of literary philosophy. Benet alludes to a wide variety of theorists as diverse as S. T. Coleridge, Edgar Allan Poe, Gustave Flaubert, I. A. Richards and Aristotle. He reveals a profound intellectual background which includes knowledge of the ancient and contemporary, Western literature and the peculiarly Spanish. Benet's essays have not as yet received the critical attention which they deserve, primarily because when he wrote them Benet was still an unknown literary figure striving for recognition. As Benet becomes a more widely accepted and respected author of prose fiction, almost certainly his theory of literature will gain the critical attention which it merits, and many of the problems discussed here will be analyzed from new perspectives.

VOLVERAS A REGION

Juan Benet attempted to publish *Volverás a Región*, his first novel, several times before it was finally accepted by Ediciones Destino in 1967. The fact that a novel by an unknown author was rejected by several publishing houses is by no means an unusual occurrence. However, it is symptomatic of the Spanish literary scene of the time that one of Benet's rejection letters included the following: "Su novela carece de diálogos. No olvide que el público lee casi exclusivamente los diálogos que suelen ser además los mejores exponentes del arte de un novelista."[1] A novel which lacked dialogue or, more precisely, a novel which was not at least partially "realistic," was alien to the contemporary trend in prose fiction. As a result, publishers chose not to risk their investments on what they believed was an unsellable product. *Volverás a Región* clearly represents, as the editors realized, a significant departure from the neorealistic novel of the 1950's and early 1960's. It exhibits several characteristics which, when analyzed in depth, exemplify an innovative approach to the novel in Spain. In the present chapter we shall investigate the uniqueness of *Volverás a Región*, and attempt to establish the intrinsic essence of Benet's novelistic reality.

What has traditionally been called the "plot" of a novel does not exist in *Volverás a Región*. Instead, the novel consists of a complex framework of third person narration and pseudo-dialogues between the two principal characters, Dr. Sebastián and Gamallo's daughter. Daniel Sebastián is an aging doctor who has been living in solitude for nearly a quarter of a century in Región, with little else to do but drink, remember and care for a child driven insane by the absence of his mother. One evening he is visited by a woman --who we know only as Gamallo's daughter-- and throughout the night the two characters carry on a soliloquy-like dialogue in which they evoke their past and examine

[1] Juan Benet, "Breve historia de *Volverás a Región*," *Revista de Occidente*, 2ª Serie, Vol. 45, N° 134 (marzo de 1974), 160-165.

their destinies. During the Civil War, the woman was the lover of Sebastián's godson (Luis I. Timoner), and this love represented for her the only happiness in her lifetime. She has returned to Región in search of the same fulfillment which she lost when Luis fled into the mountains near the end of the war. For his part, Doctor Sebastián awakens the phantasmagorical events of his past, and remembers in particular his unfulfilled passion for María Timoner, Luis's mother. Through the memories of Dr. Sebastián and his visitor, and with the additional comments of the third person narrator, we are able to reconstruct the fragmented history of the ruination of Región and its inhabitants.

Región

One of the most distinctive aspects of *Volverás a Región*, and an important element in all of Benet's novels, is the physical setting in which the action takes place. Similar to Rulfo's Comala, García Márquez's Macondo or Faulkner's Yoknapatawpha County, Benet's mythical Región plays a central role in the creation of his novelistic reality. Benet's private narrative universe --Región-- can be described in many ways. From one point of view it is the aggregate of characters, events and social themes which, in Benet's opinion, compose Spain at the time of the Civil War. However, more important than the social background is the enigmatic reality of Región itself. Benet carefully constructs the spatial and physical existence of the town on different levels of complexity. From one perspective, he portrays Región and the surrounding area with scientific preciseness. In fact, Región is described with such detail, both in its geographic and geological formation that, as Ricardo Gullón asserts, "el lector se precipita al mapa para buscar en él la ciudad y sus alrededores."[2] The mountains of Región, which is located somewhere in northwest Spain between León and Asturias, are described as follows:

La sierra de Región --2.480 metros de altitud en el

---

[2]Ricardo Gullón, "Una región laberíntica que bien pudiera llamarse España," *Insula*, Vol. 29, N° 319 (junio de 1973), 3, 10.

vértice del Monje (al decir de los geodestas que nunca lo escalaron) y 1.665 en sus puntos de paso, los collados de Socéanos y La Requerida-- se levanta como un postrer suspiro calcáreo de los Montes Aquilanos.... El encuentro de la cordillera cantábrica con el macizo galaico-portugués se produce a la manera de un estrellamiento que da lugar a la formación de esos arcos materializados en terrenos primarios que, al contacto con el sólido hipogénico, discurren en dirección NNE-SSW con una curvatura que se va incrementando a medida que descienden hacia el oeste, apoyándose en las formaciones eruptivas y cristalinas que, en dirección y convexidad opuestas, presentan sus pliegues hacia el Atlántico.[3]

Benet also strives for accuracy in the description of the *flora* and *fauna* of Región. While part of the area consists of a dry unpopulated desert, other sections near the mountains are covered with luxuriant vegetation: "Surgen allí, espaciadas y delicadas de color..., cólchicos y miosotis, cantuesos, azaleas de altura y espadañas diminutas" (p. 9). With similar emphasis on detail and exactness of description, Benet presents the rivers, valleys, deserts and mountain ranges which form Región and its vicinity.

On a second, and more complex level of reality, Benet portrays Región in a full state of decadence, surrounded by hostile landscapes and immersed in a threatening temperate zone. For example, one of the recurring images associated with Región is the labyrinth. If on the one hand Benet describes the mountains with scientific objectivity, on the other he portrays the area as a menacing maze of streams: "...en la frontera meridional que mira al este el altiplano se resuelve en una serie de pliegues irregulares de enrevesada topografía que transforman toda la cabecera en un laberinto de pequeñas cuencas" (p. 8). The traveler who attempts to reach Región by either of the two access roads encounters a similar, labyrinthine route: "El primer itinerario es penoso y laberíntico, a menudo impracticable y en algunas estaciones benig-

---

[3]Juan Benet, *Volverás a Región*, 2nd ed. (Barcelona: Ediciones Destino, 1974), pp. 36-37. Future references to *Volverás a Región* will be from this edition and denoted in the text within parentheses.

nas del año, fatal" (p. 52).[4] In contrast, yet equally as danger-
ous, the road which extends from Región to the mountains of
Mantua crosses what seems like an endless desert. As the narrator tells us in the first sentence of the novel, "Es cierto, el viajero
que saliendo de Región pretende llegar a su sierra siguiendo el
antiguo camino real --porque el moderno dejó de serlo-- se ve obligado a atravesar un pequeño y elevado desierto que parece interminable" (p. 7).

Benet paints a very complex portrait of Región, composed of
contrastive descriptions and subtle complexities. For example,
the desert --hot, lonely, hostile-- is contrasted with luxuriant
valleys nearby: "toda la vegetación que la naturaleza ha negado
a la montaña y economizado en la meseta, la ha prodigado en los
valles transversales donde se extiende y multiplica, se comprime,
magnifica y apiña transformando esas someras y angostas hon-
donadas en selvas inextricables donde crecen los frutales silves-
tres..." (p. 43). Yet despite their differences in vegetation, the
desert and the valleys represent the same impenetrable and hostile environment: "...esos estrechos y lujuriantes valles también
están desiertos, más desiertos incluso que el páramo porque
nadie ha sido lo bastante fuerte para fijarse allí" (p. 43). The
weather conditions of Región are as equally malevolent: "Porque
si la tierra es dura y el paisaje es agreste es porque el clima es
recio: un invierno tenaz que se prolonga cada año durante ocho
meses y que sólo en la primera quincena de junio levanta la mano
del castigo no tanto para conceder un momento de alivio a la víc-
tima como para hacerle comprender la inminencia del nuevo azo-
te" (p. 43). Thus throughout the early part of his novel Benet
carefully constructs an ambience in which he underscores the
hostile and contrasting elements of the physical environment:
desert-luxuriant vegetation; hot-cold; mountains-valley; rivers-
dried up streams; life-death.

On a third level of comprehension, the description of Región
stresses the mysterious and enigmatic elements which pervade

---

[4]The labyrinth is an important concept in the development of the French new
novel. According to such novelists as Nathalie Saurrate, Robbe-Grillet and
others, the world is a complex maze which the writer must portray in his novels.

the novel. In the previous chapter we have examined Benet's assertion that an author's style not only assists him in penetrating the more obscure, undefinable aspects of reality, but also aids him in the creation of new realities. In *Volverás a Región* Benet utilizes his style to break the barriers imposed by the normal perception of reality, and portrays a novelistic climate replete with mystery and ambiguity.

One of the most significant ways in which Benet creates an aura of mystery around Región is by juxtaposing antithetical elements in his description of the countryside. Whereas he meticulously describes the geological formation of a mountain or valley, he contrasts the scientific description with personification. The mountains of Región are 2,480 meters high, but the range also "se presenta como un testigo enigmático, poco conocido e inquietante de tanto desorden y tanto paroxismo" (p. 39). The mountains are alive, and can therefore witness the tragedy which unfolds both around and within them. Similarly, the rivers which flow through the valleys of Región display lifelike characteristics: "Y hacia poniente el Formigoso [el río] que, en comparación con su gemelo, observa desde su nacimiento una recta, disciplinada y ejemplar conducta para, sin necesidad de maestros, hacerse mayor de edad según el modelo establecido por su padres y recipendarios" (p. 40). Since the landscape is "alive," it not only serves as the spatial background of the novel, but also becomes an active character. Benet's descriptions of the landscape transcend the literal preciseness of the words because of their suggestive powers. The physical environment actively asserts its will and penetrates the lives of the people who live within it.

Another way in which Benet portrays the enigmatic milieu of Región is through the use of *realismo mágico*. According to Luis Leal, "En el realismo mágico los acontecimientos claves no tienen una explicación lógica o sicológica. El mágico realista no trata de copiar (como lo hacen los realistas) o de vulnerar (como lo hacen los surrealistas) la realidad circundante, sino de captar el misterio que palpita en las cosas."[5] In *Volverás a Región* Benet clearly

[5]Luis Leal, "El realismo mágico en la literatura hispanoamericana," *Cuadernos Americanos*, Año 26, Vol. 153, N° 4 (julio-agosto de 1967), 230-235.

intends to capture the mysterious elements which lie beneath surface reality. He achieves this goal in two significant ways: 1) by the juxtaposition of "real" and "unreal" elements in his description of Región; 2) through the use of specific symbolic objects which recur in the narrative, and which clearly pertain to the world of magical realism.[6]

One of the most striking elements involved in the use of magical realism is the red flower which grows wild in the mountains of Región. The flower is shaped like a chalice, and is believed to contain the blood of "todos los cristianos que a lo largo de los siglos han caído en los combates del Torce..." (p. 189). However, not only does the flower suggest a legendary past of violence, but it also plays a central role in the lives of the people who live near it: "El paisano la maldice, no la coge jamás ni la extirpa ni se atreve a llevar el ganado allá donde ella brota. El día que distraído la pisa, da un salto atrás, cae de hinojos y se persigna tantas veces cuantas floras se hallan a su vista.... Porque nace siempre donde descansa un resto humano, un hueso o un escapulario que está pidiendo venganza, recuerdo y redención al mundo de los vivos" (p. 190).

Another instance of the use of magical realism in the description of Región involves a mysterious red light, an inexplicable sound, and a painful sting, all which emanate from an unknown source. According to the narrator, for some mysterious reason --which Benet never reveals-- the traveler who attempts to penetrate the Mantuan forest begins to hear the nearby explosions of a combustion engine. Although he hunts for the source of the noise, the traveler succeeds only in exhausting himself as he frantically searches about. The same night, the tired traveler is unexpectedly awakened from his restless sleep by a bright red light. Terrified, he stares at the light, and is suddenly struck by a spear-like object which buries itself in his back and causes him great pain. (pp. 215-216) Benet explains neither the origin nor the ultimate result of such occurrences, because in fact there is no explanation. It is only one aspect of the total enigmatic reality which envelops Región and, when combined with other puzzling

---

[6]I will discuss the latter use of magical realism later in this chapter.

events, completes the intricate spatial and temporal labyrinth which Benet carefully constructs in his novel.

The Decadence of Región

The psychological and physical atmosphere of Región consists of a pervasive desolation, ruin and overwhelming fatalism. The hostile and enigmatic nature of the town permeates the inhabitants through a process of antipathetic osmosis. Similar to Juan Rulfo's Comala, there exists in Región a direct relationship between the geographical location, climatic conditions and physical ruin of the town and the ultimate abrogation of human existence. In addition, the destructive fatalism of the inhabitants of Región parallels the tragic acceptance of destiny by the people of Faulkner's Yoknapatawpha County. Both Benet and Faulkner submerge their characters in the damnatory atmosphere of moribund towns, and the result is a physical and moral human destructiveness which eventually causes complete ruination.

The inhabitants of Región do not remember when the decadence of their town first began --"La gente de Región ha optado por olvidar su propia historia"--, but it occurred at least a decade before the start of the Civil War, and is identified with lieutenant Gamallo's misfortune when in 1925 "una mujer adúltera, un donjuán de provincias y una moneda de oro sobre la mesa de juego destruyeron su carrera y arruinaron su porvenir" (p. 67). The transformation of Región did not occur instantaneously; rather it involved a creeping destructiveness which slowly permeated both the physical and psychological structure of the town. Indeed, Benet traces the prolonged decay rather than the final destruction of Región and its inhabitants. During the 1920's, for example, education in Región became part of the past: "Aun cuando la educación había caído en desuso en Región, desde la segunda década del siglo..." (p. 30). In the present time --that of the visit of Gamallo's daughter-- the buildings of Región are also in decay. Although Benet offers no detailed description of the physical condition of the town buildings, Dr. Sebastián's house symbolizes the general state of ruin: "...era una casa vieja y destartalada, carente de gusto" (p. 94); "Las paredes habían sido

--unos cuantos años atrás-- blanqueadas con cal o pintadas con temple pero las goteras y humedades habían aparecido de nuevo, impregnando todos los rincones con olor a pudrición. La pintura había saltado, algunos cristales estaban rotos y casi todos los muebles habían desaparecido tras haber dejado en la pared la huella de su espalda" (p. 118). Benet also personifies the Doctor's house: "La casa, ya lo ve usted: una construcción chapucera que a duras penas aguanta la vida media de una persona, con un olor peculiar, unas paredes que se desmoronan, un instinto, una querencia por la destrucción y la ruina" (p. 133). By attributing to the Doctor's house a will and desire for destruction, Benet intensifies the tragedy of the people of Región, and enhances the theme of a loss of desire to exist.

Another aspect of the theme of decay entails the moral disintegration brought about by increasing materialistic influences in the twentieth century. Benet vacillates on the critical point concerning the source of corruption: is it part of human nature, or does it lie within man's political and economic institutions? Although he offers no definitive answer, Benet nonetheless criticizes the importance of money and investment in modern society. As Dr. Sebastián explains, "Yo no sé --ya no lo podré saber nunca-- si es verdad que el dinero atrae el dinero; pero lo que sí puedo asegurar es que el ahorro atrae la ruina.... Y yo no sé si el dinero en sí es el demonio, lo único por lo que el hombre de este siglo está dispuesto a embrutecerse y perderse" (p. 121). Likewise, Gamallo as a youth was influenced by the greed of his two aunts. For them, "había dos palabras que predominaban sobre cualesquiera otras: dinero y hombre" (p. 69). Unlike Faulkner, for whom puritan morality and the corruption of human values was a predominant literary theme, Benet treats morality only as a minor element in his total view of Regionite society. Nonetheless, it is a significant aspect of the novel because it forms an integral part of the subtle social criticism which appears throughout.[7]

Benet's criticism of a progressive, materialistic system of

---

[7]Apart from the more obvious criticism of the Civil War and its results, Benet denounces such things as the lack of education of the poor, the fact that wealthy persons can avoid military service and the retarded development of Spain as a whole.

values is extended to all matters generally categorized under the heading of "progress." Materialism is the primary characteristic of twentieth-century society, but Benet questions the entire principle of progress: "Pues bien, no cabe duda de que el así llamado progreso se consigue a costa de algo, quizá de lo que no puede progresar; el juicio, el sano juicio, es uno de ellos, ¿no será menester sacrificarlo si hemos de andar todos al mismo paso?" (p. 222). Benet's fear of continual progress in many ways parallels Faulkner's concern for a world of increasing mechanical dehumanization. In his novel *Pylon* (1936), for example, Faulkner reveals his preoccupation with the dangers of mechanization by his portrayal of the airplane pilot as a product of speed and engines. A year earlier, Faulkner reviewed in *The American Mercury* the memoirs of a test pilot, and expressed his fears that in the future individuals would be unable to retain their human awareness and individuality. Many people, in fact, will be "forced to melt into oblivion or to unite with the representatives of blind and meaningless destruction."[8] Benet clearly shares Faulkner's concern, and through his mouthpiece, Dr. Sebastián, attempts to rationalize the value of an unprogressive society: "Es cierto que vivíamos atrasados, y ¿por qué no habíamos de hacerlo así? Y ahora nos estamos embutiendo en un disfraz sin saber cuáles eran las ventajas del antiguo vestido, sólo porque era una antigualla" (p. 222). Thus Benet asserts that, at least in part, the ruin of Región (and of twentieth-century society) can be attributed to a progressive ideal which engenders destruction and decay.

The Portrayal of Time

The presentation of time, and the correlative elements of destiny and fatalism, are inextricably bound to the principal theme of ruin in *Volverás a Región*. Although the chronological duration of the novel is only one night ("último sol de la tarde" [p. 97];

---

[8]Peter Swiggart, *The Art of Faulkner's Novels*, 3rd ed. (Austin: University of Texas Press, 1967), p. 28.

"no era aún de día cuando el Doctor despertó" [p. 312]), the psychological time spans nearly four decades, from 1925 to the unspecified present sometime during the 1960's. Through the memory of Dr. Sebastián and Gamallo's daughter we examine the past of Región and its inhabitants. However, our view of the past is not structured chronologically, but rather follows certain impulses and emotions of the characters.

Many of the great twentieth-century writers --Proust, Joyce, Dos Passos, Faulkner, Gide, Woolf-- have attempted, each in his own way, to mutilate time. Like many of these authors, Benet divides the temporal structure of his novel into several complex segments which must be reconstructed by the reader. To achieve this effect Benet frequently employs the time-shift technique, in which the temporal focus continually shifts. He deliberately fuses time periods so that the past is felt not as distinct from the present, but included in it and permeating it. In effect, past is present in *Volverás a Región*. For Benet's characters time is a fusion of present and past in which the latter is predominant. The present constantly becomes the past, while the future does not exist. In a sense, the future is decapitated by an overwhelming sense of fatalism.

The evocation of the past in *Volverás a Región* is achieved primarily through the memory of Dr. Sebastián and his visitor, Gamallo's daughter. During the course of the September evening the two characters recapture a complex, but always pessimistic past. The concept of memory itself, however, must be understood in all its perplexity. In the first place, all remembered events or feelings are distorted. As A. A. Mendilow has written concerning Proust: "...he held that the past in its purity cannot generally be recaptured because it has been modified by the experience intervening between the event and the time of the recollection, and has undergone a change in the act of passing through the crucible of the mind."[9] Benet also perceives the differences between the original act and its recaptured form. As Dr. Sebastián explains, "Es cierto que la memoria desvirtúa,

---

9A. A. Mendilow, *Time and the Novel*, 2nd ed. (New York: Humanities Press, 1965), p. 135.

agranda y exagera, pero no es sólo eso; también inventa para dar una apariencia de vivido e ido a aquello que el presente niega" (p. 247).

Memory is a patently destructive concept in *Volverás a Región*, both for the individual characters and the people of Región as a whole. For the latter, the past causes a radical devastation of their illusions, of which memory is a constant reminder: "...la memoria es un dedo tembloroso que unos años más tarde descorrerá los estores agujereados de la ventana del comedor para señalar la silueta orgullosa, temible y lejana del Monje donde, al parecer, han ido a perderse y concentrarse todas las ilusiones adolescentes..." (p. 12). Memory is as equally destructive for the individuals of the novel. It creates only solitude and despair in the young boy abandoned by his mother: "Pero hay horas sin duda en que la soledad lo es todo porque la memoria, alejada del juego [de bolas], no sabe traer sino las imágenes del hastío y los signos de aquella condición" (p. 17). For Gamallo's daughter memory is a painful reminder of a life filled with nothingness: "Porque la memoria --ahora lo veo tan claro-- es casi siempre venganza de lo que no fue --aquello que fue se graba en el cuerpo en una sustancia a donde no llegan nuestras luces.... Así que la memoria nunca me trae recuerdos; es más bien todo lo contrario, la violencia contable del olvido" (pp. 114-115). On the other hand, Gamallo's daughter occasionally exhibits a Proustian memory, for which salvation lies in time itself, in the total discovery of a vague feeling of happiness somewhere in the remote past. For this reason she has returned to Región, a fatalistic return suggested by the title of the novel: "Volverás a Región."

The concept of isolation or insulation from the world outside of Región, and therefore from time, is also an important element in the temporal construction of the novel. For the inhabitants of Región, and particularly for Dr. Sebastián, days, months and years lose their independent value and fuse into an infinite void in which time ceases to exist. Except for the events of the Civil War, past, present and future become confused, and reflect a state of complete intemporality in which time is either reduced or obliterated. For example, the black car in which Gamallo's daughter returns to Región, "no pertenece al tiempo sino a ese ayer intemporal, transformado por la futurición en un ingrávido y abortivo presente" (p. 93). The abandoned child also exists outside the limits of time in perpetual solitude, waiting for the return of his mother. In addition, the effects of the Jugador's "moneda de oro" and his final bet with Gamallo form part of an eternal mystery concerning the ruination and infinite solitude of Región: "...sólo las manecillas de un reloj barato se mueven para señalar una hora equivocada, no tanto para medir ese tiempo inmesurable y gratuito que el Jugador nos ha legado con infinita largueza como para materializar con su interminable movimiento circular la naturaleza del vacío que nos envuelve" (pp. 245-246). The presence in the novel of the child and the Jugador symbolizes the solitude and ruin of all Región. Thus for Benet, as for Faulkner and Proust, time is above all that which isolates.

The concept of time in *Volverás a Región*, like that of memory, is associated with decadence, ruination and the idea of "podría-haber-sido" (p. 95). During some moments the people of Región seem to exist in a temporal vacuum, while during others they live oppressed by the omnipresent power of time. For Dr. Sebastián time is "la dimensión en la que la persona humana sólo puede ser desgraciada.... El tiempo sólo asoma en la desdicha y así la memoria sólo es el registro del dolor. Sólo sabe hablar del destino, no lo que el hombre ha de ser sino lo distinto de lo que pretende ser. Por eso, no existe el futuro y de todo el presente sólo una parte infinitesimal no es pasado: es lo que no fue" (pp. 257-258). In effect, the people of Región (and particularly Dr. Sebastián and Gamallo's daughter) are so completely overwhelmed by the effects of time that the present ceases to exist and the future is merely a reflection of the past: "El presente ya pasó y todo lo que nos queda es lo que un día no pasó; el pasado tampoco es lo que fue, sino lo que no fue; sólo el futuro, lo que nos queda, es lo que ya ha sido" (p. 245). The Doctor and his visitor possess a past that "was not." That is, there exists nothing (or very little) from their previous life which can be remembered in a positive sense. Therefore, since their present life consists of an accumulation of past events, then in effect, there can be no hope for the future. Like the characters in Faulkner's *The Sound and the Fury*, nothing can happen to these people because everything has already happened. As one of the children declares in Faulkner's novel, "I am not is, I am was." The elusive present and nonexistent future are helpless before the character's past. As Sartre notes concerning Faulkner (but equally appropriate when applied to Benet): "Faulkner's soliloquies make us think of plane flights made rough by air pockets; at every point the consciousness of the hero falls into the past and rises once more, to fall again. The present does not exist, it becomes everything was."[10]

Benet's attitude toward time is also reflected in the form of his novel. A large portion is written in the first person, either from the point of view of Dr. Sebastián or Gamallo's daughter. In many twentieth-century novels written in the first person, there is no concept of "past" as such, but rather only a growing present. As A. A. Mendilow has shown, "No part of the past has an independent identity; the whole grows and alters as the present shifts."[11] Benet, however, achieves the opposite effect with his first person narration. His characters do not grow as a result of the fusion of past and present, but rather become stagnant. They exist to fulfill a future destiny previously determined by a ruined past. For these characters, therefore, there is no psychological distinction between chronological variations on the temporal continuum.

Benet's preoccupation with time also raises a philosophical question concerning the treatment of the consciousness of his characters. Consciousnes can be "in time," in Sartre's words, "only if it becomes time by that movement itself which makes consciousness."[12] Therefore, it is not possible to stop a man at various moments during his life and simply define him as the sum of everything he has experienced. On the contrary, the nature of consciousness implies a projection into the future. What Heidegger has called "the silent strength of the possible,"[13] can be applied negatively to Benet's novel: namely, that consciousness is not projected toward the future, but rather re-

[10]Jean-Paul Sartre, "Time in Faulkner: *The Sound and the Fury*," trans. Martine Darmon, in *Faulkner: Three Decades of Criticism*, ed. F. J. Hoffman and O. W. Vickery (New York: Harcourt, Brace and World, 1967), p. 228.

[11]Mendilow, p. 105.

[12]Sartre, p. 231.

[13]Cited in Sartre, p. 232.

gresses toward the past. For Heidegger, man is not the sum of what he has, but the totality of what he does not yet have, of what he could have. For the characters of Benet's novel, however, there exists only a pessimistic future-that-has-been. Although Dr. Sebastián is aware of and expresses Heidegger's "strength of the possible" --"Sin duda existe en nuestro cuerpo una cierta válvula defensiva gracias a la cual la razón se niega a aceptar lo irremediable, lo caducable; porque debe ser muy difícil existir si se pierde la convicción de que mientras dure la vida sus posibilidades son inagotables y casi infinitas" (p. 127)--, his own life is a poignant antithesis to his meaningless philosophizing.

Fatalism and Destiny

The principal reason for the impossibility of future fulfillment for the inhabitants of Región lies in their fatalistic concept of a ruinous, predetermined destiny. Similar to both Proust and Faulkner, Benet eliminates the dimension of free choice and action for his characters by engulfing them in an atmosphere of naturalistic positivism. Dr. Sebastián and his visitor form only one link in a chain of historical degeneration which began, as we have seen, with Lieutenant Gamallo's destruction in 1925. Benet portrays this fatalistic ruin in two significant ways: 1) through the direct philosophizing of Sebastián or the third person narrator; 2) by the use of leitmotivs and symbols associated with his use of magical realism.

Benet develops his concept of destiny and fatalism in *Volverás a Región* from the outset. Early in the novel the third person narrator declares that the inhabitants of Región often gather in the abandoned church of El Salvador to listen for shots fired in the forests of Mantua. Their reason for returning to the church remains ambiguous, except that it somehow influences their destiny: "(menos de treinta vecinos que no se hablan ni se saludan y que a duras penas se recuerdan, reunidos por un instinto común de supervivencia, exagerado por la soledad, o por un viejo ritual cuyo significado se ha perdido y en el que se representan los misterios de su predestinación)" (p. 11). From Sebastián's point of view the destiny of Región is directly related to the concept of time: "¿Y del futuro? ¿Que carecéis del futuro? Reflexionad: un futuro sólo se abre a las amenazas, todo lo demás son habladurías. Volved a casa; no os llaméis cobardes ni ruines, no ha lugar a eso porque en vuestra ruindad hay escondida toda una ciencia del destino" (p. 252). The Doctor displays, if not an understanding of his destiny, at least a passive resignation to what is required in order to survive in Región. As he explains to Gamallo's daughter in one of the few direct dialogues of the novel, "Los que vivimos en esta tierra necesitamos un plato más fuerte, una diversión más brutal." "—¿Más brutal?" "—Me refiero al fatalismo, un plato de más sustancia" (p. 128).

On one level Benet's treatment of destiny connotes a kind of nineteenth-century positivism in which the characters cannot escape from their *race*, *moment* and *milieu*. On another level, however, Benet's concept of destiny serves to intensify the mysterious world of Región and the author's attitude toward magical realism. Previously we have seen the manner in which Benet creates the complex and enigmatic ambience of Región by using certain magical elements, such as the red flower, the strange light and the bee-like sting. When treating the problem of destiny, Benet once again utilizes magical realism and, by doing so, transcends the limitations imposed by purely positivistic influences. As a result, he is able to stress the mysterious and undefinable forces at work in the decadence of Región.

One of the most striking uses of magical realism in *Volverás a Región* concerns the creation of the mysterious figure, Numa, who protects the forests and mountains of Mantua from external invasions. No one has ever seen Numa, but it is believed that he possesses omnipotent power and carries a deadly rifle as guardian of Mantua. His origins are unknown: some persons believe he is a nineteenth-century Carlist who is more than one hundred years old; others maintain that he is a monk: "hinchado de vanidad que abandona la regla cuando la intransigente reforma moderadora trata de restringir el consuelo del vino..." (p. 251). Nevertheless, no one denies Numa's existence. He forms an integral part of the mythical destruction of Región: "Lo cierto es que nadie se atreve a negar la existencia del hombre, al que nadie ha visto pero al que nadie tampoco ha podido llegar a ver y cuya imagen parece presidir y proteger los días de decadencia de esa comarca abandonada y arruinada: un anciano guarda, astuto y cruel, cubierto de lanas crudas como un pastor tártaro y calzado con abarcas de cuero, dotado del don de la ubicuidad dentro de los límites de la propiedad que recorre día y noche con los ojos cerrados" (p. 11).

Numa's existence in the novel is based upon the negation of logic and Benet's affinity for the inexplicable. His presence serves as a distressing reification of the predestined decadence of Región and the unfulfilled future of its inhabitants. Numa lives in the mountains, and is one of the mysterious shepherds "que apenas duermen" and "lo oyen todo" (p. 51). He possesses "un sentido de anticipación funeral del porvenir" and, as the narrator asks rhetorically, "Pues, ¿qué otra anticipación del porvenir que no sea la cita con la muerte cabe en esa tierra?" (p. 51).

Another use of magical realism in the determination of the future involves the telegraph wheel associated with Dr. Sebastián and his father. Both father and son feel a strange affinity toward the wheel, but the former believes firmly in its power to determine future occurrences. The wheel predicts, for example, the departure of Sebastián's father from Región and ultimately his death. For Dr. Sebastián himself, however, the telegraph has been more fatidical, because it has predetermined his entire life. Sebastián has accepted his fate --death in Región-- because he believes it is a force which cannot be thwarted: "...[mi padre] consultó a la rueda sobre mi destino y le respondió: que mis días acabarían en Región, de manera bastante violenta, en la década del 60 y en brazos de una mujer; y esa es una razón --y no la menos importante-- que me ha inducido a retirarme aquí a esperar la consumación de mi destino al cual ni me opongo ni me evado" (p. 126).

Benet's use of magical realism constitutes an integral part of the total atmosphere of ruinous fatalism in Región. Other magical elements which play a similar role include the "moneda de oro," which determines the future of both the Jugador and Gamallo, and the ethereal apparition with which Dr. Sebastián speaks at Sardu's clinic, and which is a forewarning of the death of one of his patients. The juxtaposition throughout the novel of the naturalistic-positivistic elements with the use of magical realism clearly enhances the fatalistic impact of the environment, and underscores Benet's propensity for constructing enigmatic realities.

The Civil War

Although *Volverás a Región* is by no means a social or historical novel in the manner of post-war Spanish neorealism, it contains several elements which suggest the author's social and historical preoccupations. The principal background for much of the narrative is either the Civil War itself (1936-1939), or the physical and psychological results of the conflict. In this sense, *Volverás a Región* exhibits several attributes of the historical novel as defined by G. R. Strange: "The serious historical novel... expresses a theory of history. Whatever its particular subject, it is designed to illustrate the necessary connections between the individual life and the social order, to arrive at a coherent interpretation of a significant moment of the past. In such a novel the main characters are often both individuals and representatives of historical tendencies."[14]

Benet portrays the Civil War from three points of view: the third person narrator, Dr. Sebastián and Gamallo's daughter. Each of these narrators provides a different perspective on the war, and the reader is therefore able to view the struggle from both personal and impersonal points of view. The third person narration, which begins the novel, represents Benet's most straightforward and objective prose style. When describing the actual attacks on Región by Gamallo and the Nationalist troops or when plotting the strategy of the combatants, Benet's prose frequently reads like a military manual. We are told, for example, that "los primeros combates en la Sierra de Región tuvieron lugar a comienzos del otoño del año 1936, como consecuencia de los ataques llevados a cabo contra los pueblos de la vertiente oriental de la cordillera, por unos pocos insurrectos de Macerta" (pp. 27-28). In a similar, direct manner the third person narrator

---

[14]G. R. Strange, "Introduction" to William Makepeace Thackeray, *The History of Henry Edmond, Esq.* (New York: Holt, Rinehart & Winston, 1962), p. xv.

relates the unsuccessful attacks against Región in 1937, and the eventual conquest of the town by Nationalist forces in 1938. Few details are spared, and the military strategy of both sides is depicted in the novel as if on a map. The same narrator also introduces several minor characters, such as Eugenio Mazón, Constantino, Asián and Julián Fernández, all members of the Región militia who defended their town against the invading Nationalists, but who were ultimately forced to flee into the mountains of Mantua. The intellectual, Aurelio Rumbal (or Rombal, Robal, Rembel, Rubal, Rumbas, we never learn which is correct), is also presented in his capacity as philosophical leader of the Región forces. Although Rumbal plays a relatively small role in the novel, his symbolic significance cannot be overlooked as the intellectual man of words, but not action.

The events associated with Región during the Civil War represent a microcosm of the conflict on the entire peninsula. In the first place, the Región militia are a heterogeneous group of nonsoldiers, a fact which is symbolized by the disparity in their dress and arms and by the disagreement concerning their military strategy. Consequently, the type of combat in Región reflects the fighting in all of Spain: "Todo el curso de la guerra civil en la comarca de Región empieza a verse claro cuando se comprende que, en más de un aspecto, es un paradigma a escala menor y a un ritmo más lento de los sucesos peninsulares; su desarrollo se asemeja al despliegue de imágenes saltarinas de esa película que al ser proyectada a una velocidad más lenta que la idónea pierde intensidad, colorido y contrastes" (p. 75). More important, however, is the fact that the people of Región became Republicans at the outset of the war for no particular ideological or political reasons: "Fue republicana por olvido u omisión, revolucionaria de oído y belicosa no por ánimo de revancha hacia un orden secular opresivo sino por coraje y candor, nacidos de una condición natural aciaga y aburrida" (p. 76). As a political force the Regionites were "una especie de parlamento sin gobierno que se hallaba muy lejos de poder salir al paso de las desavenencias y decisiones personales" (p. 84). Thus, from the perspective of the third person narrator, the role of the Regionite people in the Civil War may be summarized as follows: they are a group of disorganized militia, who do not know why they are involved in the war, and who are incapable of overcoming the differences in their personal desires for the good of the town. Taken as a whole, they represent Republican forces throughout Spain.

For Dr. Sebastián, the Civil War is an event which arouses philosophical speculation. Unlike the objective, third person narrator, Sebastián is inclined to analyze the origins or outcome of war, while dedicating scant attention to historical facts. He never mentions specific dates, nor does he concern himself with the actual combat of the conflict. Instead, he subsumes the war within the general time frame of "past," and relates it to the recurrent themes of decadence and despair.

While the thirty years since the Civil War have produced perpetual decay in Spain (from a social perspective the dissolution of Región symbolizes the ruin of Spain under Franco's rule), the period prior to the war offered no positive alternatives. Although Dr. Sebastián claims not to understand the historical complexities of the pre-war years, he offers his personal view concerning the origins of the struggle: "Lo que sí creo es que cuando una sociedad ha alcanzado ese grado de desorientación que llega incluso a anular su instinto de supervivencia, espontáneamente crea por sí misma un equilibrio de fuerzas antagónicas que al entrar en colisión destruyen toda su reserva de energías para buscar un estado de paz -en la extinción-- más permanente" (p. 184). Therefore, the Civil War was not fought for constructive purposes, but for destructive ones. There were few praiseworthy aspects to pre-war Spanish society, no hope for the present or the future. As Dr. Sebastián asks, "¿Por qué no volver al terreno del odio? Sólo de la derrota podría surgir algo nuevo; no ha sido así, pero eso no quita nada al hecho de que fuera la mejor razón para hacer la guerra: poderla perder" (p. 159).

Extinction, destruction and ruin are the primary elements of Sebastián's frame of reference, and all events from the past or present are included within these categories. The Civil War is no exception: "Es lo que queda de aquel entonces, voces, suspiros, unos pocos disparos al final del verano... es todo el alimento de nuestra postguerra; vivimos del rumor y nos alimentamos de cábalas pero nuestro momento ha pasado, ha pasado para siempre" (p. 245). Dr. Sebastián is effectively incapable of perceiving life in any other way. He is submerged (like post-war Spain) in his own solitude, overcome by Time. His opportunity to obtain meaning in life "ha pasado para siempre."

The third point of view expressed on the Civil War is that of Gamallo's daughter. The now middle-aged woman perceives the war neither as an objective set of historical facts, nor as a subject for detached, philosophical abstractions. Rather, the war for her is fused with both personal tragedy and happiness. On the one hand, the war represents a loss of innocence and a sudden maturation for the then young girl. She experiences her first love affair during the war but, in contrast, was also raped for the first time. She endured great anguish, yet also discovered the plenitude of life with her lover, Luis I. Timoner. In the end, however, as occurs with all things associated with Región and the war, her life has been destroyed, and she is condemned to a future-that-has-been: "Apenas me enteré de aquella guerra sino cuando ya estaba terminando. Algo tarde, en algo más que una semana sufrí todas sus consecuencias: un padre muerto, un amante desaparecido, una educación hecha trizas, un conocimiento del amor que me incapacitaba para cualquier futuro..." (p. 159).

Although the Civil War is not the principal point of departure in *Volverás a Región*, it plays a central role in the dominant theme of ruin which recurs in different forms throughout the novel. All that remains for the people of Región after the war is an overwhelming sense of defeat; not a military defeat (although they did lose Región to the Nationalists), but rather an acceptance of their own ruin and despair. The process of decay in Región originated several years prior to the war, and the armed conflict merely hastens and intensifies this process. In the words of Gamallo's daughter, Región and its inhabitants are incapable of experiencing "cualquier futuro."

Instinct and Reason

The pessimistic point of view which pervades *Volverás a Región* stems in large part from the primordial conflict between the two antithetical elements of man's being: instinct and reason. The struggle between these two factors is a psychological constant in the novel, and is directly related both to the ruination of the two major characters and to Spain as a whole.

In the conflict between reason and instinct Benet, like Freud (whose influence is manifest throughout the novel), views the latter as the dominant force. Reason is the enemy of man *qua* man in his instinctual essence, a fact which is symbolized by many of society's institutions. The family, for example, comes under rigorous attack by Dr. Sebastián: "Es [la familia] la verdadera trampa de la razón: un animal rapaz que vive en un nivel diferente al del hombre..." (p. 137). The family exists "on a different level" than man because, as a societal institution, it was created by reason and is therefore harmful to man's primordial being. Furthermore, the moral and behavioral codes of society "son redactados por la razón, un aparato al que apenas le interesa lo que el hombre es y desea" (p. 139). It is thus impossible for a human being to develop his essential being --instinct-- because of the repressiveness of the society in which he lives.

According to Freud, the basic mental conflict of man is created as a result of societal norms: instinctual tendencies must either be excluded from consciousness and action (as in repression), or modified (as in sublimation). In *Volverás a Región*, the latter alternative is chosen by Dr. Sebastián's wife, who sublimates her sexual desires into a sort of mystic purity during her twenty years of marriage to the Doctor. In contrast, Gamallo's daughter is forced into an inescapable labyrinth of guilt and desire, because the free gratification of her instinctual need is incompatible with civilized society. Her psychological destruction is a result of, on the one hand, her abandonment to instinctual passion and the release of innate desires, while on the other being forced to search for nonexistent rational justification for her actions. Ultimately, reason triumphs: she has returned to Región guided by an instinctual impulse to seek pleasure, but the rational victory of society is symbolized by her death.

The fundamental conflict which Benet establishes between instinct and reason on a personal level can be expanded to include the nature of society as a whole. There exists no solution to the perpetual struggle between the two opposing forces, and thus the psychological state of society can be described as the collective "daily unhappiness" of its members. In effect, the history of man is the history of his repression. As Herbert Marcuse notes

64

concerning the theories of Freud: "Civilization begins when the primary objective --namely, integral satisfaction of needs-- is effectively renounced."[15] In *Volverás a Región* Dr. Sebastián and Gamallo's daughter are palpably aware of this conflict, and are therefore condemned to suffer. As Alberto Oliart affirms, Dr. Sebastián and his visitor submerge themselves "cada vez más en la degradación de su condición, ayudados por el alcohol, o quieren romper la cadena de su propia condición y encuentran la muerte, porque la sociedad-razón no perdona a los que quieren trastocar el orden establecido, a los que intentan negar su condición humana y cambiarla."[16]

Style

It is evident from our earlier discussion of *La inspiración y el estilo* that for Benet, style is the essential element of all prose fiction. Once a writer has acquired a highly developed style, he is able to transcend the purely "informational" aspects of his novel --i.e., plot, setting, characters-- and thereby produce a novel of more lasting value. Furthermore, a fully developed style is important because it is the writer's main instrument for the creation of his novelistic reality. For Benet the world is a complex enigma which the writer must penetrate and subsequently portray in his novels. In order to be successful, the writer must utilize his chosen medium --language-- as a means of discovery. The greater the facility with which the author manipulates language --*viz.*, the more developed is his style-- the more perceptive will be his discovery: "Yo creo que ante una situación así el hombre de letras no tiene otra salida que la creación de un estilo. Ninguna barrera puede prevalecer contra el estilo siendo así que se trata del esfuerzo del escritor por romper un cerco mucho más estrecho, permanente, y rigoroso: aquél que le impone el dictado de

[15]Herbert Marcuse, *Eros and Civilization* (Boston: Beacon Press, 1966), p. 11.

[16]Alberto Oliart, "Viaje a Región," *Revista de Occidente*, 2ª Serie, Vol. 27, Nº 80 (noviembre de 1970), 224-234.

la realidad."[17] However, not only does the writer discover the mysteries of his surroundings, but he also invents reality through the skillful use of language: "La realidad se presenta ante el escritor bajo un doble cariz: es acoso y es campo de acción. Mientras el escritor no cuenta con un instrumento para dominarla se ve acosado por ella; pero un día su cerco es perforado y toda su inmensa y compacta hueste pasa a formar parte de las filas del artista y a engrosar sus efectivos.... De forma que el enemigo --aquella realidad indefinible e infinita-- se torna ahora su aliado. ¿Qué barreras pueden prevalecer contra un hombre que en lo sucesivo será capaz de inventar la realidad?"[18]

Concerning the literary style of William Faulkner, Warren Beck has written: "If Faulkner's sentences sometimes soar and circle involved and prolonged, if his scenes become halls of mirrors repeating tableaux in a progressive magnification, if echoes multiply into dissonance of infinite overtones, it is because the meanings his stories unfold are complex, mysterious, obscure and incomplete."[19] The preceding quote by Beck is as equally appropriate in our discussion of Benet's style in *Volverás a Región*. Form and content are tightly interwoven in Benet's novel and, taken together, form the complex reality of Región and its inhabitants.

In *Volverás a Región* Benet employs two dissimilar styles of writing. In his portrayal of the Civil War, or in the scientific descriptions of Región, he utilizes a straightforward, direct prose which manifests a concern for detail and accuracy. Each geological explanation or description of the *flora* and *fauna* is carefully expressed, and Benet displays an intimate knowledge of scientific terminology. In contrast, when describing the enigmatic elements of Región, and especially in the lengthy soliloquys of Dr. Sebastián or Gamallo's daughter, Benet utilizes a very complex, highly metaphorical language which in many ways resembles the

[17]Juan Benet, *La inspiración y el estilo* (Madrid: Revista de Occidente, 1966), p. 160.

[18]Juan Benet, *La inspiración y el estilo*, p. 160.

[19]William Beck, "William Faulkner's Style," in *Faulkner: Four Decades of Criticism*, ed. L. W. Wagner (East Lansing: Michigan State University Press, 1973), pp. 141-154.

style of Faulkner. Frequently Benet's complicated syntax is as impenetrable as the mysterious mountains of Mantua.

Benet's style, "un estilo laberíntico," according to Ricardo Gullón,[20] is part of his whole elaborate method of creating his novelistic reality. His sentences are frequently the length of a full page or more, and include parentheses, parentheses within parentheses and subordinate clauses which unite to form a syntactical webwork. Benet's style is, in fact, a persistent maze of obstacles replete with complex obtrusions, delays, ambiguous interpolations and confusions. Benet's purpose in creating such difficulties is two-fold, depending upon the narrative point of view. When used by the third person narrator, for example, the baroque-like sentences increase the enigmatic nature of the reality he is attempting to create. The mere length of the sentences seems to be part of a deliberate plan to withhold the meaning he hopes to convey: the partial or delayed disclosure of the central idea of a sentence often occurs near the end, thus keeping the reader intrigued (and confused) until the last instant.

Because of his peculiar style of writing Benet's characters are essentially stylized creations. The monologues of Dr. Sebastián and Gamallo's daughter are the antithesis of realistic speech patterns, and serve to dehumanize the characters. The use of esoteric vocabulary and, conversely, the total lack of common word choice, further diminishes the realistic nature of the characters. Nevertheless, Benet overcomes the shortcomings of stylized characters by stressing the tragic human problems which consume them. Benet's ability at psychological analysis is in no way undermined by his style. On the contrary, the depth of his characters is enhanced by the complexity of their monologues and the details of their descriptions. Benet's characters do not aspire to speak succinctly because, in the words of Dr. Sebastián, "el sustantivo se me escapa" (p. 182). That is, the ideas or emotions which the characters express are so complex that a single noun or short descriptive phrase is rejected in favor of a more peripatetic pattern of speech. The result is a highly artificial soliloquy in which Benet nonetheless achieves psychological depth. As War-

20Gullón, p. 10.

ren Beck notes concerning a similar problem in Faulkner: "There is no absolute, no eternal pure white radiance in such presentations, but rather the stain of many colors, refracted and shifting in kaleidoscopic suspension about the center of man's enigmatic behavior and fate..."[21]

The symbiotic relationship between the material decadence of Región and the destruction of the characters is also enhanced by Benet's style. Frequently Benet makes a direct comparison between the physical decay of a character and a material object. When describing Dr. Sebastián's house, for example, the narrator suggests that "La misma humedad que había destruido la pintura, podrido la madera y levantado el piso, parecía haber afectado al timbre de voz del doctor" (p. 118). Likewise, María Timoner is compared to the withered leaves of the black poplar tree: "Rodeada de sombras su cara --y su silueta-- parecía haberse fundido con la pared que en la oscuridad aun guardaba cierta coloración purpúrea de las últimas luces de la tarde, de la misma tonalidad que las hojas marchitas de los chopos que cubrían el antepecho de la ventana" (p. 136).

Benet also uses a number of leitmotivs in his novels. Both the fragmentary nature of the narrative and the ambiguity of certain events are affected by this treatment: the first, because the appearance of recurrent symbols at the beginning of a new section in the novel facilitates the reader's understanding of the section, and brings into focus certain associations which recur throughout the work. Such is the case, for example, with the appearance of the black car, which suggests specific incidents related to Gamallo's daughter and the abandonment of the child. Likewise, the mention of the "camioneta" evokes the flight and subsequent rape of Gamallo's daughter during the war; or the "moneda de oro," which alludes to certain incidents and themes associated with the Jugador and the ruin of Gamallo and Región. The use of leitmotivs also intensifies the dehumanization of the characters. Benet rarely refers to the characters by their name, but instead suggests their presence by using certain images. Gamallo, for

[21]Beck, p. 152.

example, is frequently represented by his emaciated hand, and the presence of María Timoner is often symbolized by her engagement ring. Likewise, the abandoned child is never given a name, but is associated with thick-lensed glasses. By repeatedly using these symbols Benet enhances his stylistic intention of suggesting realities instead of naming them directly. Benet's circumlocutions form the salient characteristic of his complex style, and the slow, indecisive manner of much of his writing becomes his principal tool in the creation of both the physical and psychological reality of his novel.

Although Juan Benet first created Región in his collection of short stories, *Nunca llegarás a nada* (1961), the mythical town does not reach full development until the publication of *Volverás a Región*, in which its geographic and enigmatic peculiarities are presented in detail. The people of Región, to whom Benet deliberately attributes a mysterious, ethereal type of existence, do not actually form a real society. Yet they are significantly related to a real society and their mythic history is related to real history. In fact, Región and its environment transcend national boundaries and symbolize the whole existential predicament of the twentieth century. Indeed, much of Benet's success in *Volverás a Región* can be explained in terms of his ability to express universal themes by means of stylized characters, without detracting from the dramatic force and mythical realism of his narrative situations.

There can be little doubt that William Faulkner significantly influenced the writing of *Volverás a Región* in several ways: Benet's preoccupation with time, the creation of a hermetic novelistic reality, the themes of decay, ruin and solitude and the author's peripatetic style all suggest Faulknerian influence. In addition, Benet quotes Faulkner near the end of the novel and indicates his source in a footnote.[22] Geographically speaking, Región differs substantially from Faulkner's Yoknapatawpha County. On a thematic level, however, a naturalistic positivism and destructive fatalism pervade the atmosphere of both envi-

---

[22] "[los ladridos] irreales, sonoros y regulares, timbrados por esa triste y resignada desolación," p. 290.

ronments, and rigidly control the characters' lives.

Benet's temporal preoccupations are manifest throughout his novel. As we have seen previously, the inhabitants of Región are submerged in a timeless void in which past, present and future are fused to form a meaningless existence. In relation to time, Benet's character portrayal is clearly antithetical to Bergson's theory of *durée*, upon which much of twentieth-century character development depends. Basically, Bergson contends that every individual living form is the continuation of an indefinite past in a living present. Personality is viewed as a process of continual renewal in which the ever-present past plays an active role. During the twentieth century this theory of *durée* has caused a progressive narrowing of the fictional duration covered by a novel, at the same time that the psychological duration of the characters has expanded. In *Volverás a Región*, however, although the psychological time is much greater than the chronological duration, the characters experience no internal growth. Dr. Sebastián and Gamallo's daughter live in a moment when their consciousness still exists, but when time has been forever stopped. Their present and future consist only of a ruinous past.

In *Volverás a Región* Benet develops a highly complex narrative structure. He utilizes a carefully constructed style in order to portray mysterious elements of both reality and unreality. His novel represents an explicit rejection of post-war realism and *costumbrismo* in favor of a Faulknerian milieu and memory. Although social criticism exists in the novel, it is subordinated to stylistic, structural and temporal concerns, as we have discussed above. Benet does not attempt to reproduce contemporary Spanish society in his work, but he succeeds in portraying on a mythical level, in Ricardo Gullón's words: "Una Región laberíntica que bien pudiera llamarse España."

UNA MEDITACION

Una meditación, Juan Benet's second novel, was awarded the prestigious Premio Biblioteca Breve in 1969 by Editorial Seix Barral.[1] Although the novel displays certain stylistic and philosophical characteristics evident in *Volverás a Región*, it represents a more ambitious undertaking than Benet's first novel. Written in the first person, *Una meditación* is precisely what the title suggests: a meditation on the past which covers a time span of nearly fifty years from 1920 to the present. Although the novel is composed of an artistically manipulated structure (i.e., not a loosely formed stream of consciousness), the events and characters which are presented do not appear in a specific, chronological arrangement. Instead, the narrator evokes a succession of fragmented memories which frequently remain vague and incomplete. The novel consists of one long paragraph, a feature which Benet stressed by submitting it to the publishers on a long, unbroken roll of paper rather than in the normal fashion of sequentially typed pages. The linear, uncut nature of the manuscript, however, by no means resembles the internal structure and content of the novel. Utilizing a Proustian memory and a Faulknerian style, the narrator scrutinizes the past in an attempt to recover and understand the nature of his family, friends and previous existence in the vicinity of Región.

The traditional use of plot, which in *Volverás a Región* is reduced to a minimum, regains significance in *Una meditación*. However, there is no dramatic development and subsequent denouement, and the novel could easily be rearranged without detracting from the intrinsic interest of the events themselves. As the narrator's mind wanders through the past, certain incidents and characters are summoned into consciousness and placed in view of the reader. No single event or character, however, is pre-

---

[1]Other well-known winners of the Premio Biblioteca Breve include Mario Vargas Llosa, *La ciudad y los perros*, 1962; Guillermo Cabrera Infante, *Tres tristes tigres*, 1964; Juan Marsé, *Ultimas tardes con Teresa*, 1965; Carlos Fuentes, *Cambio de piel*, 1966.

sented in its entirety during a specific moment in the novel. Instead, Benet creates a complex labyrinth of interpenetrating segments which represent the narrator's voluntary and involuntary
memory and the desire for a "remembrance of things past."
Since Benet presented the geographic formation of Región in
great detail in his first novel, there was no need to repeat the process in *Una meditación*. However, the reader who is familiar with
Volverás a Región cannot help but be influenced by his previous
knowledge of Región upon reading *Una meditación*. In the same
way that our familiarity with Yoknapatawpha County influences
our reaction to the novels of William Faulkner, our knowledge of
the mythical Región affects our reading of subsequent novels
which take place in the same location. This is especially true in
Una meditación, because Benet repeatedly refers to places, characters and events which appeared in his earlier novel. Dr. Sebastián ("ya de joven enlutado, tan alto y con cabeza de visiona-
rio"),[2] for example, reappears as Mary's doctor. Reference is
also made to Numa, Gamallo, "la Muerte" (the owner of the
inn), as well as to several Regionite family names associated with
the Civil War. In addition, although the action of *Una meditación*
does not occur directly within Región proper, the town is frequently mentioned and the same atmosphere of ruinous destruction pervades the novel: Región is described as "momificada, en-
vuelta en podredumbre, hastío, soledad" (p. 242). A mountain-
ous area near Región is as equally hostile and sterile in its mere
appearance: "No, no es que el Hurd tenga mucho de particular;
es un escudo de rocas ácidas, sombrío y estéril, que estructura y
deforma los últimos valles de montaña del Torce antes de abrirse
paso hacia el mioceno de las mesetas" (p. 273). Beyond the Torce, of course, lie the desert-like areas leading toward the impenetrable forest of Mantua, which is also mentioned several times in
Una meditación.
Although Benet does not discuss the Civil War in great detail
in *Una meditación*, the conflict nonetheless plays an important

---

[2]Juan Benet, *Una meditación* (Barcelona: Editorial Seix Barral, 1970), p. 37.
Future references to *Una meditación* will be from this edition and denoted in the
text within parentheses.

role in the prevailing atmosphere of ruin and decay. When the narrator returns to Región in 1939, the destructive effects of the war are everywhere manifest:

> (estaban abiertas todas las heridas de la guerra, un buen número de casas --las que seguían de pie-- vacías, abandonadas u ocupadas por gente desconocida, las familias divididas y dispersas, muchos de los nombres de mi primera juventud pronunciados con encono, otros eran poco menos que innombrables si se quería dormir en paz, un ánimo inquieto, vengativo y malévolo prevalecía en todos los triunfadores que todos los días, a todas las horas y en todas las esquinas alardeaban de su victoria para lo que no era suficiente glorificar su gesta sino que necesitaban cubrir de insultos a su adversario como si recelosos e inseguros de su triunfo sin decidirse a bajar la guardia y dispuestos a enarbolar en todo momento las banderas, las razones, las armas y los principios que les movieron a la lucha, necesitaran todavía mantener la contienda con la palabra, ese recurso final cuando la acción es impotente, y una estela de rencor, menosprecio y cierta indiferencia que dejó el barco que se llevó a todos los derrotados, ansiosos de tener entre sí y sus hermanos un océano cuando menos).... (p. 63)

Several of the narrator's memories concern events which take place after the war, and the country is described in terms of a diseased body which has unsuccessfully attempted to cure itself: "Si el espíritu de postguerra fue o quiso ser una convalencia pronto se había de convertir en un nuevo mal que... se hizo endémico como vino a demostrar --sólo para aquel que viviera allende de las fronteras pues no había en España una persona tan ajena a su influencia como para establecer el diagnóstico en oposición a su propio pronóstico-- el resultado que obró sobre aquel cuerpo enfermo y mutilado por la guerra el conjunto de numerosas, horrendas y paralizantes medicinas que le fueron suministradas en la paz que siguió" (p. 88). Thus from a social perspective, which most critics incorrectly find completely absent from Benet's novels, Franco's government has magnified certain economic and social problems, but more importantly, has infused Spanish society with a paralytic state of mind in which the inability to think or to act has resulted in the continual deterioration of the nation's spiritual and physical condition.

The theme of *soledad* also reappears in *Una meditación*. As we have seen in our study of *Volverás a Región*, the inhabitants of Región, and especially Dr. Sebastián, live overwhelmed by a tragic sense of solitude and despair. In *Una meditación* the theme is treated explicitly only on occasion, but is implicit in the actions of the characters who seek fulfillment in their lives. In one of the direct references to solitude, the narrator describes his parents as "distantes, repentinamente jóvenes y graves y aislados del resto de la familia, [y] una vez más parecían reducidos a una soledad que conocían de sobra, que el nacimiento y educación de sus hijos había disimulado durante unos pocos años..." (p. 48). In general, however, the themes of solitude and isolation are associated with the characters in terms of sex and love, while the search for a meaningful existence depends upon establishing a lasting erotic relationship through love and affection.[3]

Structure and Technique

Benet's use of a first person narrator in *Una meditación* creates several structural and temporal problems in the development of the narrative. In the first place, whenever we encounter the "I" of any novel, we are conscious of an experiencing mind whose views of the experience come between us and the event. The "unreliable" nature of a first person narrator has been analyzed at length by Wayne C. Booth,[4] and we will therefore not attempt to study it here as a theoretical problem. Benet himself, however, has stressed the complex nature of his first person narrator in *Una meditación*, and has pointed out the ambiguity caused by presenting a limited point of view: "Este discurso es la memoria de un señor, que es un joven antes de la guerra, y vive

---

[3]The treatment of sex and love in *Una meditación* suggests a definite Freudian influence in the novel. I will discuss this aspect in detail later in the present chapter.

[4]See Wayne C. Booth's well-known study *The Rhetoric of Fiction* (Chicago & London: University of Chicago Press, 1970).

en un país imaginario que tiene un parentesco geográfico con Región.... Este señor se equivoca, confunde y, sobre todo, como todo narrador de muchas cosas, no dice la verdad y produce en su propio discurso sus insidias y, por lo tanto, se contradice."[5]

The "I" of *Una meditación* infrequently discusses his own personality and rarely indulges in self-analysis. Nonetheless, the personality of the "I" is implicit in everything that he relates. First of all, the "I" plays an important role in the theme of "the return," which is explicit in the title of Benet's first novel, and is underscored in *Una meditación* by the return to Región of several of the characters: Mary, Carlos, Leo and the narrator himself. All the characters have returned to Región in search of something, and the narrator is no exception: "Casi todo lo que ahora trato de traer a mis ojos tiene ese cariz, no como consecuencia de la ruina sino a causa de la memoria; debe ser la facultad de toda especie dolida, que necesita saber en parte lo que fue --o contar en sustitución del conocimiento de un paliativo engañoso-- para vencer el dolor que le produce lo que es" (p. 52). The whole narrative method of the "I" takes root in his desire to recapture the past (i.e., to return psychologically to Región) as a means of explaining the present. Each major event which he relates is followed (or interrupted) by a lengthy digression on the subject at hand. Even the most reticent narrator becomes dramatized automatically as soon as he refers to himself as "I." In *Una meditación*, although the digressions are generally externally directed, they nonetheless reveal certain of the "I's" own personality traits. His constant preoccupation with such recurring topics as sex, ruin and time, and the numerous philosophical observations which he offers concerning these subjects, all serve to characterize a particular point of view (and personality) through which the events of the novel are filtered.

One of the fundamental aspects of the first person narration in *Una meditación* is the peculiar perspective provided on certain incidents of the narrator's life. During the early parts of the novel the narrator relates several events from his childhood, all of which are presented in the same manner and tone as those of his

[5]Antonio Núñez, "Encuentro con Juan Benet," *Insula*, Vol. 24, N° 269 (abril de 1969), 4.

adulthood. In contrast to Dickens' *Great Expectations*, for example, where the narrator, Pip, grows and matures as the narrative develops, the narrative tone of *Una meditación* remains the same throughout. Although the "I" successfully portrays a penetrating view of childhood ideas and emotions, it is always in the form of a detached, intellectual digression from the main narrative stream. In fact, the narrator seems to make a conscious effort not to filter the events through the eyes of a child, but rather through the mind of a remembering adult. Such is the case in the following examples:

> En ciertos años de la vida del niño el mayor atractivo que la vida le ofrece se cifra en la mudanza de algunas cosas porque, no habiendo adquirido todavía el apego a las costumbres, apenas sabe deleitarse con la reiteración periódica de un placer que sólo debe repetirse en la medida que no agote el tanto de sorpresa que conlleva. (p. 19)

> ...el niño educado en el rigor cada vez que percibe en sus padres un motivo de preocupación del cual él no es la causa, siente una suerte de alivio que le lleva incluso a desdeñar la importancia del asunto y a suponer, por ignorancia, que una guerra civil no se puede comparar en cuanto a su trascendencia con la rotura de la luna de un armario o una herida en la cabeza de un hermano pequeño. (p. 47)

> Durante unos cuantos años el niño (o acaso era antes) acepta el universo de los adultos como algo sustancialmente ajeno a él, las más de sus leyes incomprensibles, las más de sus figuras hieráticas, casi inmóviles, que apenas explican las razones de su mutismo y malhumor, que sólo de tarde en tarde dejan asomar un aspecto amable para dar a entender que aun perteneciendo a la misma especie un accidente insoslayable e irreconocible los ha apartado para siempre de la familia infantil. (p. 69)

In effect, many of these digressions read as if they were excerpts from a psychological manual on child behavior. It is evident, therefore, that Benet's concern lies not with passing childhood events through the consciousness of a child, but rather with filtering these events through the cognitive processes of meditation and adult reflection. As the narrator himself observes: "(y ahora con los años se me antoja mucho más evidente..." (p. 17). That is, the adult perspective explains the childhood behavior.

The "I" of *Una meditación* is what Wayne C. Booth would categorize as a "narrator-observer,"[6] and therefore is conscious of his role as the conveyor of information within a preconceived narrative structure. Frequently, the "I" intrudes in the narrative in order to express his control over the telling of the story and the order of events: "Los detractores de tal doctrina (el más apasionado de ellos era mi tío Alfonso del que, si viene al caso, se hablará más adelante)..." (p. 170). The "I" is also aware of himself as a source of factual information, and occasionally expresses concern for his manner of narrating. In one instance he explains why he has included a detailed description of Cayetano Corral: "Si cuento todos estos detalles no es tanto con el propósito de buscar una ficticia y solamente relativa amenidad como espoleado por el deseo de dar a conocer algunos particulares de aquel hombre" (p. 77). In contrast, the "I" is conscious of his fallibility as a narrator. Since he experiences a strong desire to tell the truth --"Aunque hubiera preferido cualquier otra explicación me veo obligado a suponer que..." (p. 78)-- he readily admits that he cannot remember certain events: "Y por si fuera poco tenía un nombre que yo no he conocido otro más solemne aunque lo he olvidado" (p. 21); "Pero uno de nosotros --no recuerdo quién, era muy pequeño..." (p. 24); "...yo no recuerdo --no lo visualizo-- haberme despedido de él" (p. 50). The narrator, therefore, expresses his concern for accuracy of description and confesses his shortcomings as a recorder of past events.

Despite the efforts of the "I" to define his limitations --"¿Cómo voy a saber de qué manera se inició aquella conversación?" (p. 199); "Parece que..." (p. 155); "¿Fue ese talante tan flemático lo que le llevó a cerrar un trato con el Indio? No lo diré" (p. 275)-- the descriptions and analyses of characters in *Una meditación* frequently reflect the view of a third person omniscient narrator who relates the thoughts and motives of his characters. Be-

---

[6]Wayne C. Booth, p. 153.

net attempts to legitimize in part the omniscience of the "I"[7] by placing him in certain situations where he can see or hear events, or by making him an acquaintance of a particular character. Such is the case, for example, when the "I" attends the homage to Jorge Ruan and encounters Mary, Carlos and Cayetano; or when he relates the events he observed as a child in his grandfather's house. The presence of the narrator allows him to witness the events directly and therefore relate them in a straightforward manner as narrator-observer. However, in contrast to the usual limitations of the first person narrator, the "I" of *Una meditación* becomes the center of consciousness not only for external, observable occurrences, but also for the psychological development of the other characters. The frequency with which the "I" presents glimpses into the consciousness and private lives of the characters introduces an artificial note into the narrative, and detracts from the verisimilitude of the entire "meditation."

Nonetheless, there are several advantages to the omniscient "I." In *Una meditación* the omniscience is used frequently as a means of controlling dramatic irony through straightforward description. For example, Leo feels disgust for Emilio after their insipid lovemaking at the inn. Emilio, on the other hand, misinterprets completely his relationship with Leo and the reason for their sexual involvement. The misinterpretation is something only an omniscient narrator could know, since it consists of Emilio's private judgments and Leo's private motives. Yet the scene would be pointless as a clue to the personality of the two characters unless the misjudgment were made clear to us. In this situation, therefore, the "I" has adapted his role to the narrative circumstances and has presented privileged information normally associated with a third person narrator.[8]

---

[7]The term "first person omniscience," which at first seems to be contradictory, is by no means original when applied to Juan Benet. See, for example, B. G. Rogers' study *Proust's Narrative Techniques* (Geneva: Librairie Droz, 1965), for a detailed analysis of this narrative method.

[8]Benet also uses dramatic irony within the limitations imposed by a first person narrator. Such is the case, for example, in the humorous episode of the grandfather's liquor. The "I" is aware of the fact that his uncle has substituted "Port Said" for the grandfather's more potent whiskey. Since the grandfather receives great pleasure from watching others suffer when having to drink his powerful

In addition to the portrayal of dramatic irony, Benet employs the omniscient first person narrator for two important purposes: 1) to describe events which occur outside the frame of reference of the "I"; 2) for the psychological development of several of the characters. The first of these roles of the omniscient "I" recurs throughout the novel and serves to broaden the informational base of the work. Examples of this technique include the episode between Rufino and Emilio Ruiz at the mine, Leo and Carlos' trip into the mountains and frequent descriptions of the sexual activities of various characters within the confines of their rooms. The detailed descriptions of these and other events serve to undermine the effectiveness of the first person narration in the novel. Since the purpose of the narrative structure is to recapture the past through the memory of one individual (and therefore necessarily to present a subjective view of the past), then the objective presentation of certain past incidents by means of third person omniscience detracts from the overall effect of using a first person narrator with a limited frame of reference.

Although first person narration is used frequently in fiction as a means of self-analysis, the very nature of the technique generally prohibits its use in analyzing the inner thoughts of other characters. In *Una meditación* the narrator is frequently undermined by the pseudo-subjective point of view which he imparts. Not only does he relate external actions to which he has no possible access, but he also attempts to penetrate the characters' minds and portray their private thoughts. When describing the relationship between Jorge and Camila, for example, the "I" explains that, "[Jorge] había llegado a ver en Camila (y a verlo en toda su oquedad) el vaciado del otro yo, cuya última naturaleza estaba tan lejos de poder sospechar; sabía que mientras su padre viviera en casa --acumulando datos para incrementar el vasto material de la 'Descripción de los muros,' sin avanzar un paso en

---

liquid, his ignorance of the substituted liquor becomes the butt of the joke as narrated by the "I." The ironic humor of the situation is increased by the contrast between the narrator's awareness of the substitution and the grandfather's complete confidence in his whiskey. The entire episode, however, lies within the direct experience of the narrator and therefore is distinct from the omniscience displayed in the love-making of Leo and Emilio.

80

la redacción-- no podría volver a escribir un verso..." (p. 275).
Likewise, when describing the consequences of Leo's return to
Región, the narrator exceeds the potential limits of his knowledge: "Pero cuando tras un par de meses en Región [Leo] se dio
cuenta en su cruda realidad de la soledad de su nueva *demeure*,
sin el consuelo o apoyo de un par de amistades firmes y perma-
nentes, por fuerza vino a considerar si aquella decisión tan lúcida
no tenía también sus zonas de sombra..." (p. 190). Thus psychological development in *Una meditación* frequently depends upon
the omnipresent mind of the narrator.

Occasionally Benet demonstrates a preoccupation with expanding his narrative point of view. Instead of depending upon
the "I" for a paraphrase or opinion, Benet inserts the viewpoint
of the original source. For example, when discussing the reac-
tions of the people of Región to the early days of the Civil War,
the narration switches to the direct discourse of Tío Ricardo (pp.
40-47). By means of this lengthy monologue Benet achieves a
new perspective in the novel without resorting to first person
omniscience. Likewise, when Leo and Carlos journey into the
mountains, Cayetano Corral sends a letter to Carlos, which is re-
produced in part within the narrative. The effect of the letter is
similar to that of Ricardo's monologue: it offers a break in the
first person narration which allows Benet, while ostensibly doing
no more than reproducing certain thoughts of a character, to
vary the narrative viewpoint while dispensing with an external
or even implicit narrator.

Time and Memory

Benet's treatment of time and memory in *Una meditación*
clearly resembles the temporal concerns evident in *Volverás a
Región*. In both novels time plays an integral part in the psychological and physical ruin of Región and its inhabitants, and
serves as a point of departure for philosophical speculation. In
Una meditación, however, the reflections on time by the first
person narrator are actually reflections on the writing of the
novel itself. Since the novel consists of the recollection and subsequent expression of past events, any kind of temporal specula-

tion must necessarily reflect on the construction of the work. Thus time and recollection, which form the intrinsic essence of *Una meditación*, play an equal role in both the form and content of the novel.

Although the concept of memory is examined in detail in *Volverás a Región*, it performs a more vital function in the overall development of *Una meditación*. In the latter novel, the first person narrator makes a conscious effort to recover certain elements of the past, but the events which he is able to recollect and the distorted chronological order in which they enter his mind are beyond his rational control. Benet does not question the ability of memory to receive and record the events and ideas of the human experience. In fact, he affirms the power of the memory: "Nunca he comprendido cómo la desaparición temporal del recuerdo se achaca al olvido, desmentido por tantos fenómenos, porque de la misma manera que la roca sedimentaria guarda en su seno todas las huellas de los seres que dejaron su impronta cuando tan sólo era un légamo blando e impresionable, así la memoria puede cobijar y atesorar todo lo que en su día tuvo la consistencia necesaria para dejar un rastro indeleble" (p. 29). On the other hand, memory may be viewed as a *mélange* formed by equal parts of remembering and forgetting. On the question of summoning into memory many of the "forgotten" events, Benet vacillates between the powers of reason and sensation. The title of the novel suggests that the former provides the principal impetus: a rational, self-probing reflection or meditation can recover (at least partially) the past. Within the novel, however, the philosophical digressions of the "I" undermine the title. Although a concerted effort to stimulate the memory is useful (and perhaps necessary), the "I" strongly suggests that it is the involuntary memory, the free association of ideas, which recreates the past:

> El día en que se produce esa inexplicable e involuntaria emersión del recuerdo, toda una zona de penumbra, que parecía olvidada y sobre la que el afán de conocer había perdido todo estímulo --tras una renuncia obligada por su incapacidad para superar la voluntad de ignorancia--, empieza a ser iluminada tibiamente; y tanto más se esclarecen las líneas de aquel instante

preciso --en apariencia deformado pero en rigor con-
servado intacto por el mismo olvido que lo envolvió
durante tanto tiempo-- tanto más se cierran las tinieblas cronológicas que lo rodean, rompiendo esa pre-
tendida continuidad de un pasado que no es un tiempo dimensional sino un conjunto infinito y limitado de
quietos instantes de luz en un continuo oscuro y mó-
vil. Para la memoria no hay continuidad en ningún
momento: una banda de tiempo oculto es devorada
por el cuerpo y convertida en una serie de fragmentos
dispersos, por obra del espíritu.... Así se produce un
relato fragmentario y desordenado que salta en el
tiempo y en el espacio, que acumula datos, imágenes
e impresiones.... (pp. 31-32)

The conception of time in *Una meditación* closely parallels the
notion of temporality expressed by Michel Butor in *L'Emploi du
Temps*: "Ainsi la succession primaire des jours anciens non nous
est jamais rendue qu'à travers une multitude d'autres, change-
antes, chaque évènement faisant en résonner d'autres antérieurs
qui en sont l'origine, l'explication, ou l'homologue, chaque mo-
nument, chaque objet, chaque image nous renvoyent à d'autres
périodes qu'il est nécessaire de ranimer pour y retrouver le secret
perdu de leur puissance bonne ou mauvaise, d'autres périodes
souvent lointaines et oubliées...."[9] With Butor, however, the re-
awakened past may contain "good or evil," while for Benet the
past is always destructive. That is, the past consists of those
things that did not occur, and therefore predestines an empty future. This theme, which recurs throughout Benet's first novel,
reappears in *Una meditación* with equal significance: "¿Lo re-
cuerdas? Pero aquello ya pasó y sólo queda lo que no fue" (p.
321).

While memory provides the means for examining or recovering
the past, the whole notion of time --past, present and future-- is
carefully analyzed in *Una meditación* and embodies a fundamental thematic preoccupation. Clearly, Benet rejects a "mathematical" view of time[10] in favor of a more vital, flowing concept as

[9]Michel Butor, *L'Emploi du Temps* (Paris: Les Editions de Minuit, 1957), pp.
294-295.

[10]Bergson defined mathematical time (as opposed to *durée*) as the temporal re-

expressed in Bergson's theory of *durée*. According to the French philosopher, change is an integral aspect in the existence of a living being. The one things of which we may be completely certain is a constant flow, or Duration. This concept, which forms the central principle of Bergson's overall philosophy, may be defined as "the continuous progress of the past which gnaws into the future."[11] Since man is a living being, he belongs to the stream of duration and, as Bergson claims, "If we attend sufficiently closely to our own experience, we can become conscious of the pulsing of Duration within us."[12] Benet's *Una meditación* is a complex affirmation of this theory. The narrator's meditation coincides with Bergson's insistence that we can "attend sufficiently closely to our own experience." As the "I" in Benet's novel asserts, the memory can attempt to recover "esas imágenes tópicas envolventes de los mil caminos y las mil tardes y los cientos de domingos --todos parecidos y ninguno semejante-- que constituyen nuestro andar" (pp. 30-31).

In addition to the temporal elements involved in the structure of *Una meditación* (i.e., the continual amassing of fragmented memories), time is treated concretely in the form of Cayetano Corral's clock, and in abstraction by means of the narrator's numerous digressions. The clock, which has been in Cayetano's possession for several years, does not run. Although he has worked on the clock ever since he has owned it, his preoccupation is not with fixing, but with "perfecting" the machine: "...durante años se dedicó a renovar y perfeccionar hasta el punto que del ejemplar original sólo habían de quedar los elementos estáticos" (p. 77). In effect, Cayetano aspires to gain a complete understanding of the concept of time, both in its "mathematical" and

---

lation which we interpose between material things. C. E. M. Joad explains the concept as follows: "If we consider any material thing which passes through two successive states and then double the rapidity of succession we will in no way affect the reality or the nature of the states, nor of the material thing which passes through the states.... Time, then, as science conceives it, is not part of the material world." From *Guide to Philosophy* (New York: Dover Publications, 1946), pp. 548-549.

[11]C. E. M. Joad, p. 549.

[12]C. E. M. Joad, p. 549.

"durational" essence. However, like everything else he has attempted, he fails to perfect the enigmatic clock: "Y como suele ocurrir --y con qué frecuencia se repite ese ejemplo, tanto en una actividad tan inocente como aquella como en cualquier otra, mucho más ambiciosa-- aquel reloj --y todos los objetos mecánicos a los que dedicó su afición-- no sirvió más que como modelo... de una otra cosa que a la postre nunca llegó a hacer" (pp. 77-78).

The principal function of the clock is to underscore the ruin and destruction of the characters and, by extension, of all of Spain after the Civil War. The characters exist in a type of paralytic stupor in which time has stopped. The future, therefore, does not exist. As the "I" notes in one of his digressions:

¿Qué puedo encontrar que me sirva de clave para encontrar la razón --ya no la justificación-- ni de ser lo que fui ni lo que esperé, ni de poder esperar ya otra cosa que no ser nada ni al menos poderme anticipar al no ser nada para ser algo dejando de ser nada? De la misma forma que cuando insistía con mis furtivas miradas al reloj, sus manecillas parecían detenerse como si jugaran conmigo a un cruel escondite y trataran --con esa muda e impenetrable malignidad de los mecanismos-- de persuadirme de la inmovilidad en que estaba radicado pese a mis esfuerzos por avanzar en la dirección cronológica del tiempo.... (pp. 65-66)

The silence of the clock symbolizes the total absence of meaning in the people's lives. The inhabitants of Región have no "potentialities," in Heidegger's terms, as a means of escaping their temporal vacuum. Thus the clock "marca con su silencio el compás de espera entre vida y existencia" (p. 74). Similar to *Volverás a Región*, then, Benet's *Una meditación* reveals the author's concern for portraying time as that which isolates and destroys.

The clock attains additional significance through the use of personification and the subsequent revelation of its thought processes. During the years when Cayetano was working to perfect the clock (i.e., trying to gain an understanding of time), the instrument in effect lay dormant. However, when Leo departs for the mountains with Carlos Bonaval, Cayetano suddenly becomes obsessed and attempts to repair the clock as quickly as possible. As the clock is adjusted (as it grows closer to being alive, symbolized by its ticking), the narrator penetrates its thoughts and makes them available to the reader. Psychological time, believes the clock, brings about much more destruction than the mere chronological flow of events. Referring to Leo's arrival from America and her subsequent effect on Cayetano, the "I" tells us that "...él (reloj) que habría podido medir el tiempo... consumido en aquella espalda reclinada sobre el banco para llevar a cabo su reparación, era quien mejor sabía cómo el tiempo es mucho más grávido cuando es advertido y cómo las horas que transcurrieron en un espasmo, en un susto o en un santiamén, nunca dejan de pasar la cuenta en largos momentos de supina incredulidad e inmitigable tedio.... El tiempo era ahora más real, más absoluto, más independiente de las manos y del celo del amo, completamente ajeno a la capacidad métrica del reloj; más ruinoso, por ende, más aciago..." (p. 81). Time is not measured by the rhythmic pulsating of the clock's moving parts, but by the mechanism of the human psyche: "...solamente los desastres y las pasiones son capaces de fijar el tiempo" (p. 203); "...el tiempo no se engendró ni en las estrellas ni en los relojes sino en las lágrimas" (p. 71).

The setting into motion of the clock is associated with the unloosing of the latent destructive destiny of the characters. The clock itself becomes the prophet of future tragedy and the ticking represents the "comienzo de la edad nefasta" (p. 81). The pulsating grows more intense and its sound (i.e., the releasing of the destructive force of time) expands to the town of Región and into the surrounding mountains:

> Un latido anormal fue tomando cuerpo y creciendo, si no en sonido al menos en resonancia, extendiéndose por el cobertizo, por el patio y por el almacén de la fábrica, provocando la caída y rotura de muchos platos y ollas apiladas que, sin el menor aviso, se vinieron abajo pulverizadas antes de tocar el suelo; luego se extendió a los alrededores, a toda Región y su sierra, y toda su comarca sacudida por aquel lejano y acompasado golpe que no cesaba ni de día ni de noche, que apenas se oía... pero que poco a poco, al parecer, iba debilitando y agrietando fundamentos y cumbreras, provocando pequeñas desportilladuras y esas caídas de polvo blancuzco que manchan los sue-

86

> los, los manteles y los platos para anunciar la inminencia de la catástrofe. (p. 288)

The universalization of the ticking clock magnifies the themes of ruin and damnation which pervade *Una meditación*, and accords time the omnipotent power of destruction.

Eros, Love and Sex

Eros and sexual desire constitute a recurrent topic of concern in *Una meditación*, and are treated both in the abstract during the philosophical digressions of the "I," and concretely through the portrayal of several of the characters.[13] Love and sex furnish the motivating forces behind many of the occurrences in the novel, and Freudian influence can be noted throughout. As we have seen in our earlier study of *Volverás a Región*, the conflict between reason and instinct, and the repression or sublimation of the latter, forms the nucleus of Freud's theory of civilization. Those who attempt to fulfill their instinctual desires are ultimately overcome by the rational nature of society and, as occurred with Dr. Sebastián and Gamallo's daughter, are condemned and punished. In *Una meditación* Benet expands his treatment of reason and instinct, and intensifies the sexual desires of his characters to such a degree that eros and frustrated emptiness become synonymous with sex and life itself.

[13]Freud distinguishes between the terms Eros, sex and love in his *An Outline of Psycho-Analysis* (trans. James Strachey [New York: W. W. Norton, 1969]). Eros is one of man's basic instincts, and is counterbalanced by the death instinct, later designated Thanatos. As Freud writes: "After long hesitancies and vacillations we have decided to assume the existence of only two basic instincts, *Eros* and *the death instinct*.... The aim of the first of these basic instincts is to establish ever greater unities and to preserve them thus --in short, to bind together; the aim of the second is, on the contrary, to undo connections and so to destroy things" (p. 5). The sexual function, according to Freud, is merely one manifestation of libido, the total available energy of Eros. Love results only when "the main quota of libido is transferred on to the object [e.g., another person] and the object to some extent takes the place of the ego" (p. 8). I have used each of these three terms because they appear in *Una meditación* as important factors in the development of characters and theme.

According to Freud, non-repressive order in society is possible only if the sex instincts can generate lasting erotic relations among mature individuals. Since society must maintain strict control over sex instincts, any genuine decrease in this control would reverse the organization of sexuality toward precivilized stages. As Herbert Marcuse has written concerning this problem: "Such regression would break through the central fortifications of the performance principle.... Under the performance principle, the libidinal cathexis of the individual body and libidinal relations with others are normally confined to leisure time and directed to the preparation and execution of genital intercourse."[14] In *Una meditación* the cathexes of various characters are directed toward an always elusive sexual fulfillment by means of genital intercourse. Such is the case with Leo, who has experienced several sexual affairs in her life, none of which produced "lasting erotic relations." During her trip with Carlos Bonaval, for example, "Dos o tres días de intimidad bastaban para reducirla a sus constantes básicas; una mezcla de coraje y falta de bravura, un mal disimulado por la curiosidad horror a la soledad pero sobre todo la cruda necesidad primigenia de una pasión concluyente cuyo recio aroma guardaba su cuerpo y su piel despedía con el primer contacto carnal.... Pero con una vida resuelta y sin excesivos compromisos, en su manera de conducirse despreocupada y libre había algo que sonaba a hueco y en lo que el menos avisado podría advertir la oscura premonición de una evolución que desembocaba en hastío, soledad y deriva" (p. 317). Leo's sex instinct is not inhibited in its aim, and therefore violates Freud's theory of lasting interpersonal relations upon which civilization (and personal happiness within society) depends. Leo fails to obtain the desired fulfillment which --as with nearly all personality traits associated with Freudian psychology-- "[es] derivada del hecho de no haber alcanzado nunca un fin buscado desde la adolescencia" (p. 85).

If sexual gratification eludes the characters of *Una meditación* as a means of obtaining permanent satisfaction, the sexual act itself provides a temporary liberation from the obstacles which

[14]Herbert Marcuse, *Eros and Civilization* (Boston: Beacon Press, 1966), p. 199.

prevent fulfillment. The most important of these is the constant oppression of time: the characters repeatedly attempt to reawaken the past and analyze their life-that-has-been. This desire to recover the past is one of the archetypical means of gaining happiness. As Marcuse notes: "From the myth of Orpheus to the novel of Proust, happiness and freedom have been linked with the idea of the recapture of time: the *temps retrouvé*."[15] In *Una meditación*, however, eros is used as a means of defeating time in a world which essentially is dominated by time. According to the narrator, "la adhesión amorosa destemporaliza el tiempo" (p. 311). That is, the chronological time of the sexual act (i.e., the discharge of instinctual psychic energy) creates a psychological period of escape during which time exercises no influence. In effect, sex conquers time, but only temporarily. After orgasm we begin "la vuelta a la conciencia que, tras el acto de amor, exige la reanudación del ciclo crónico después de la evaporación del espíritu y la reducción de la carne a duración. La eternidad concluye; el tiempo vuelve a andar para devorar de nuevo su propio ser escondido ya en el pecho del hombre de donde asomó un instante en el culmen del orgasmo para devorar a su criatura predilecta al tiempo que era castrado por ella convertida en un instante flotante... en esa ocasión calva e inaprensible, ausente de toda temporalidad" (p. 294).

Through his sexual gratification, claims Freud, man becomes a higher being, committed to higher values than the primordial urges associated with pure instincts. The sexuality of man is dignified by love --i.e., sexuality with affection.[16] In *Una meditación*, however, Benet debases the Freudian theory of love and sexuality by frequently reducing the characters to their animalistic, instinctual drives. Benet achieves this effect in two significant ways: 1) by the creation of similes and metaphors in which human beings are compared to animals; 2) by using Freudian related sex symbols, through which the characters' sex drives are related to animalistic imagery.[17]

---

[15]Herbert Marcuse, p. 199.

[16]Herbert Marcuse, p. 199.

[17]I will discuss Benet's use of animalistic metaphors and similes later in this chapter in the context of style and language usage.

During one of his digressions the narrator discusses the human being in relation to primitive animals: "Si con algo cuenta el alma es con ese sistema rudimentario, ese residuo de la red nerviosa de un primitivo animal cuya figura se ha extinguido pero cuya influencia, como la de cualquier precursor, se deja sentir bajo la piel de todo hombre" (p. 139). Translated into Freudian terminology, the sex drive is part of the instinctual energy used in service of life (as opposed to the death instinct, *thanatos*). In Benet's novel, however, the sex instinct is never sublimated into a form of libidinal work within society, but rather always remains in its primitive stage of pure desire. This attitude is evident in particular in the relationship between Jorge and Camila: "Aunque dispares y emotivamente inocuos tenían en común cierta inefable perversidad, esa remota e inaprensible categoría del animal que tras siglos de domesticidad cobija un núcleo indomable que sólo asoma, a ratos en sus guiños o en sus bostezos..." (p. 257). For her part, Camila is described in terms of her animal-like strangeness, as an alien in a civilized society: "...en realidad [Camila] estaba animada de imperceptibles vibraciones, minúsculos ruidos y crujidos orgánicos que salían de un interior que debía padecer una permanente y frenética actividad delatando la indomeñable naturaleza que no sabía de otra forma protestar de su larga permanencia entre la sociedad de las personas civilizadas" (p. 259).

The sexual relationship between Jorge and Camila is the most deviant of the novel. In part, the sexual contact of the two characters can be defined according to Jorge's rivalry with his father. The two Ruan's do not maintain a close relationship, and the reason for Señor Ruan's mysterious hostility toward Jorge's accomplishments is never made totally clear. Jorge, however, compensates for the antagonism between him and his father by pursuing Camila, thereby fulfilling his obvious Oedipus complex. In addition, however, the constant association of Camila with cats and Jorge's perverse pleasure in torturing rats emphasize the grotesque intimacy between the two, and serves to dehumanize their sexual desires.[18]

[18]Camila's association with cats, of course, also enhances the mysterious, solitary nature of her personality.

Jorge's fetish for rats is linked to an incident which occurred when he was young. The water pipe leading into his house became blocked, and the family hired the foreman of the coal mine (Rufino) to fix the pipes. After working for a short while Rufino inserted his hand into the pipe in order to remove what he believed was the final obstacle. But instead of clearing the pipe, Rufino painfully withdrew his hand on which a rat had tightly clamped its teeth. The foreman responded quickly, however, and bit the neck of the rat until the animal was dead. Meanwhile, Jorge, who was watching Rufino work, had grown pale and "arrojaba todo lo que había en su estómago" (p. 265). This incident with the foreman becomes critical in the novel because it explains a large part of Jorge's sexual behavior with Camila. The rat symbolizes the female vagina or, by extension, the maternal love absent in Jorge's life. The pipe, on the other hand, is an obvious phallic symbol which represents the male penis. When Jorge and Camila make love the rat, which serves as an erotic symbol for Jorge, is replaced by Camila: "Poco a poco... había de sustituir el cuerpo de Camila al de la rata" (p. 266). In the same manner which the foreman bit the jugular vein of the rat, Jorge bites the earlobe of the prostitute until he draws blood: "luego le mordió el lóbulo de la oreja --intensamente, hasta sentir que sus dientes entraban en contacto, separados por un velo-- y cuando --ciega, sorda por su propia jadear e incapaz de llamarle por su nombre, ascendiendo en la cerúlea claridad del orgasmo-- sintió que su sangre corría por su mejilla... se retiró de la habitación, tras dejar en la almohada el cadáver de una rata que hasta entonces había ocultado en un bolsillo de su pesado abrigo de lana cruda" (pp. 143-144). When Jorge leaves the dead rat on the pillow, Benet leaves no doubt as to the symbolic significance of the animal: "[la mujer de Brabante]... tomó el cadáver de la rata y lo acarició repetidas veces para al fin depositarlo, hecho un ovillo, sobre las mantas justamente encima de su sexo" (p. 144). The sexual relationship between Jorge and Camila represents, therefore, the antithesis of what Freud would consider a "higher form of sexual gratification." The two lovers display a purely erotic desire to fulfill instinctual needs, and Benet effectively vitiates their relationship through his use of animalistic imagery and symbols.

The portrayal of Emilio Ruiz offers another example of instinctual sex desires. Emilio's sex complexes originated during the Civil War, and his efforts to fulfill his instinctual desires lead him only to failure. He is rejected by Leo, by the woman from Belgium who stays at the inn and even by the female owner/ prostitute of the inn. In order to release his frustrated desires, Emilio waits each night outside of the prostitute's room until he reaches orgasm, "tras el cual [vuelve] a su cuarto caminando a cuatro patas" (p. 135). Cayetano Corral also discharges his sexual energies in a deviant manner. Basically, Cayetano is a masochist. When not unbridling his energy upon women --"Y en cuanto a mujeres solamente de tarde en tarde --y lo que es más singular, solía encontrarlos-- le atraían los monstruos" (p. 75)-- he spends time "castigando al cuerpo" (p. 75). The goal of sexual consumation is replaced by a need to suffer, and Cayetano achieves masochistic pain by swimming until his body becomes numb: "Era un gran nadador... aunque de ninguna manera encontraba el menor placer en practicar tal deporte al que dedicaba muchas horas del día, durante las así llamadas vacaciones, para castigar al cuerpo" (p. 75). Thus Cayetano Corral, Emilio Ruiz, Jorge, Camila, Carlos, Leo and other characters of *Una meditación* exist in perpetual frustration. Through genital intercourse they are able to release libidinal energy in its most primitive form, but none of the characters is able to achieve the happiness and fulfillment of lasting erotic relations based upon love and affection. As the narrator remarks concerning Leo, but which is applicable to nearly all the characters: "Yo no dudo de que para esos amantes inveterados existe también un principio de sinceridad, buena fe y un afán por alcanzar de una vez el fin tantas veces perseguido y nunca logrado, cuando se embarcan en una nueva aventura; si algo se les puede reprochar es precisamente esa ceguera a que voluntariamente se dejan arrastrar tanto por su ingenuidad como por un hábito para el que es más fácil llevar a cabo una nueva intentona que deducir la ley en virtud de la cual todas se traducen en fracasos" (p. 83).

Style

Benet's style of writing in *Una meditación*, although similar to that of *Volverás a Región*, is much more complex. Written in a single paragraph which extends for 329 pages, the novel demands the reader's active participation in penetrating the baroque syntax and untangling the complicated system of images. Although *Una meditación* resembles Proust's *A la Recherche du Temps Perdu* in terms of narrative structure and technique, the influence of Faulkner remains predominant in Benet's complex style of writing. Like the American writer, Benet frequently amasses words in a manner which has caused some critics to charge him with prolixity. Indeed, many of Benet's sentences cover several pages, and it becomes a difficult task to remain attentive to the assorted ideas contained in one of the narrator's thought patterns. On the other hand, Benet's peripatetic style can be justified because of its intimate association with the content and structure of the novel. As Warren Beck has written concerning Faulkner, but applied with equal accuracy to Benet: "In his most characteristic writing Faulkner is trying to render the transcendent life of the mind, the crowded composite of associative and analytical consciousness which expands the vibrant movement into the reaches of all time, simultaneously observing, remembering, interpreting and modifying the object of its awareness. To this end the sentence as a rhetorical unit is made to hold diverse yet related elements in a sort of saturated solution, which is perhaps the nearest that language as the instrument of fiction can come to the instantaneous complexities of consciousness itself."[19] Like Faulkner's, Benet's sentences are perhaps best described as "saturated solutions" in which diverse images and topics are juxtaposed in order to create complex and enigmatic realities.

One of the recurring characteristics of Benet's style in *Una meditación* is his presentation of opposed or contradictory suggestions within a single context. Similar to Faulkner's use of oxymoronic or near oxymoronic terms in many of his novels,[20]

[19]Warren Beck, "William Faulkner's Style," in *Faulkner: Four Decades of Criticism*, ed. L. W. Wagner (East Lansing: Michigan State University Press, 1973), p. 152.

[20]See Walter Slatoff's study, "The Edge of Order: The Pattern of Faulkner's Rhetoric," in *Faulkner: Four Decades of Criticism*, *op. cit.*

Benet utilizes the contradictory statements to maintain his novel in a state of flux or suspension, thereby keeping the reader confused and uncertain in his response. The oxymoronic descriptions which Benet employs are constructed by the simultaneous suggestions of disparate or opposed elements, and therefore create a sharp polarity or tension. For example, when Leo and Carlos visit the Indio's hut, Benet creates an atmosphere of fear and mystery. The two travelers enter the hut and hear "un ligero crujido de peldaños y un suspiro ahogado, cercano y lejano a la vez" (p. 160). The relationship between Mary and Carlos after several years of separation is described as "esa relación que une y separa a la vez al hombre formado y maduro con un primer apunte hecho en su juventud" (p. 225). When examining the potentially destructive results of Cayetano Corral's scientific investigations, the narrator concludes that "nada parecía más imposible y remoto y al mismo tiempo más inminente" (p. 281). Or, as a final example, when discussing Leo's inner self during her affair with Carlos, the narrator claims that Leo's "[yo]... era al mismo tiempo aniquilado y engendrado" (p. 291). As a result of these contrastive descriptions, Benet achieves a kind of order and coherence by virtue of the clear and sharp antitheses which the contrasts involve. On the other hand, such descriptions create disorder and incoherence by virtue of their qualities of irresolution and contradiction. Thus the use of oxymoronic description can be viewed as an integral part of Benet's desire to keep the reader from piecing things together in a perfect and orderly fashion. The paradoxical nature of the oxymoronic relationship keeps many aspects of Benet's novel insoluble.

Walter Slatoff's conclusion that full coherence in Faulkner's novels is something the author hoped to avoid can also be applied to Benet's *Una meditación*. The distorted time sequences, the juxtaposition of largely independent stories and the unsyntactical marathon sentences all indicate an eagerness to avoid order and coherence. Benet constantly imposes obstacles to the complete and rational comprehension of events by his experiments with both style and content. He chooses to suggest complex, enigmatic realities rather than define circumstances which are orderly and unequivocal.

Although the total impression which Benet conveys in *Una*

meditación is one of ambiguity and abstruseness, the metaphorical system which he employs is based on concrete comparisons and exactness of description. As we have seen in our earlier discussion of Benet's theory of the metaphor (chapter II), Benet insists that the two components of metaphoric expression (tenor and vehicle) must be sufficiently concrete so that the accuracy of the statement is in no way diminished and the desired meaning is thus conveyed. As he remarks in an interview with Miguel Fernández-Braso: "...la metáfora cumple su función si el segundo término de la comparación es muy real. La metáfora en los poetas de la época helénica tenía, originariamente, un propósito metafórico claro y didáctico. Mostraban sus conceptos con ejemplos derivados del mundo natural. Hoy, siguiendo esa misma función, es preciso retraer la función primordial de la metáfora a un mundo dominado por la técnica y la civilización moderna."[21]

Benet's use of concrete metaphoric description is manifest throughout *Una meditación*. One of the most frequently used types of metaphor incorporates scientific images and terminology. For example, when describing the approach of a car on the dusty road to Región, the narrator declares that "...la maligna topografía hacía coincidir el sonido inconfundible del motor con la nubecilla de polvo que poco a poco se va agigantando para descubrir en su centro --como el foco del microscopio al despejar la nebulosa tornasolada y reducirla a la celda en cuyo interior se mueve el tímido virus-- el punto negro que tras un primer instante inmoble se agranda envuelto en su penacho de iridiscente pulvición..." (p. 131). When commenting on the manner in which certain experiences remain hidden within our memory, the narrator claims: "[hay] otras que apenas dejan residuo en ella [la memoria], durante las que se está consolidando la costra dura del individuo, de la misma manera que en un mismo instante geológico la zona que estuvo sumergida en un agua saturada de vida animal aparecerá cuajada de fósiles en contraste con aquella otra... que sometida al régimen regresivo de desecación aparecerá exenta de señales de vida, cubierta tan sólo de cal, sílice o

---

[21]Miguel Fernández-Braso, "Juan Benet: un talento excitado," in *De escritor a escritor* (Barcelona: Editorial Taber, 1970), pp. 201-202.

yeso" (p. 32). The history of Spain (and of all civilization) is also explained with scientific terminology: "la historia no es más que un modo de ser que lleva cada sociedad que elige como medio de perpetuarse un proceso interminable de evolución y transformación... así que para vivir en la historia es preciso consumir y devorarse, transformar recursos en energía y ésta a su vez en disipación del calor hasta alcanzar la neutralización de los niveles energéticos" (p. 89). Benet's predilection for scientific allusions can be explained in part by biographical data: his training as an engineer has undoubtedly molded his perspective to conform with the demands of his profession. From a literary viewpoint, however, the concreteness of his scientific imagery supports his theoretical assumptions concerning the origin and role of metaphoric expression. On the other hand, this precise vocabulary stands in sharp contrast to the subjective mode of narration and the distortive process in which the narrator's mind is constantly engaged.

Another important stylistic device in *Una meditación* involves the use of animalistic imagery to dehumanize the characters. Camila, as we have seen, is repeatedly ascribed feline characteristics and never gains full development as an actual human being: "[tenía] una cualidad impenetrable e inconsciente... y algo felina también, como si tras sus pupilas dormitara un animal que producido por toda la sabiduría de la naturaleza no hubiera llegado a alcanzar la reflexión, quedándose en ese contradictorio nivel inferior, protegido de los achaques y debilidades de la consciencia" (p. 257). Likewise, Jorge is dehumanized due to both his sexual intimacy with Camila and the imagery associated with him as an individual. His hostile feelings toward his father, for example, are portrayed as follows: "su hijo [Jorge] supo esperar sereno y amenazador, como el animal que con sólo adoptar la actitud de defensa, irguiendo la cabeza y adelantando el pecho, sabe disuadir a su enemigo de lanzar el ataque" (p. 231). Benet's use of animalistic imagery to describe some of his characters, coupled with the stylized manner of narration and dialogue and the ambitious nature of much of the action, combine to create essentially dehumanized and abstract characters. As one reviewer has remarked concerning *Una meditación*: "Benet --escritor amigo de la cosificación-- raras veces logra deparar la sensación de vida, sangre y calor."[22] However, although the characters do not appear to be "de carne y hueso," the problems with which they are associated are palpably real: sex, the escape from time, memory, despair. Thus Benet's "dehumanized" characters struggle with "human" problems characteristic of all mankind.

The hostile environment which Benet meticulously portrays in *Volverás a Región* reappears, although with less intensity, in *Una meditación*. In contrast to the dehumanized characters, the physical environment is frequently personified. The inhabitants of Región are submerged in a destructive atmosphere which is "alive," and displays a particular personality. The valley which lies beyond the bridge, for example, "espera aún de los hombres una suerte de redención a la penitencia impuesta por una tectónica frustratriz que, atenta tan sólo a la compensación isostática de las grandes masas, olvida con frecuencia el equilibrio y la armonía de las formaciones de segundo orden" (p. 150). The sky of Región emits "el silencioso bostezo de un cielo fatigado y pesaroso que envuelto en un halo húmedo presiente su vergüenza y reprime sus lágrimas con un gesto esquivo, reclamaran para sí el tributo fúnebre que el hombre reserva para el reino animal" (p. 57). The decadent condition of Región is also emphasized through personification: "...y la caída --tanto tiempo diferida, anhelada y temida-- de un terrón de césped que desprendido del ribazo se desploma de un golpe-- como si en el último instante hubiera tenido que elegir, tras muchas vacilaciones, entre la azarosa travesía y la permanencia en una tierra que amenaza con su descomposición-- para disolverse en ocre torbellino de partículas sueltas" (p. 57). The active role of the spatial environment thus plays an integral part in the intrinsic reality of *Una meditación* by enhancing the theme of ruin and intensifying the mysterious and enigmatic nature which permeates the novel.

Benet employs a number of leitmotivs and recurring symbols in *Una meditación*. Frequently, the leitmotivs influence the fragmented narrative structure by enhancing the ambiguity of certain situations which are not clarified until later in the novel.

Such is the case, for example, with the recurring image of the rat. When Mary becomes ill and moves in with the Ruan family, the narrator inserts a passing reference to rats: "[Mary] no demostraba demasiada repugnancia por el juego de las ratas" (p. 110). At this stage of the novel the reader is still unaware of the important role which the rat plays in the perverted sexual needs of Jorge. However, as the novel develops the rat acquires symbolic importance due to its recurring appearance in situations which involve sex. Only after we learn that Jorge is obsessed with rats do we discover that it was he who entered the prostitute's room at the inn and left the dead rat on the woman's pillow. Thus the initial scene with the prostitute, which occurs on page 144, remains ambiguous until nearly a hundred pages later when the narrator informs us that Jorge could not sleep because of the rats pattering about above the ceiling of his bedroom (p. 232). Later, we learn that Jorge links Camila and the rat in his fantasies of making love, and finally we are told the reason for Jorge's fixation on rats (pp. 264-265). This intricate structuring of the novel based upon a leitmotiv enhances Benet's overall stylistic purpose of ambiguity. By withholding the explanation of the importance of the rat Benet effectively achieves his goal of suggesting rather than naming realities.

Another important symbol concerns Mary's dark glasses. When staying with the Ruan family during her illness, Mary constantly wears the glasses: "...sentada [Mary] en el centro del jardín en un sillón de mimbre, protegida por sus gafas" (p. 110). As she grows more ill and approaches death the narrator uses the glasses to portray her changing state of health: "...las gafas que parecían crecer a medida que su salud se deterioraba y su cara se reducía" (p. 111). When Mary finally dies, her death is symbolized by her broken glasses: "[Mary] murió en la hamaca, junto a las gafas caídas y rotas" (p. 111); and later: "[Mary] murió --en pleno verano y en pleno tarde-- con la única sacudida enérgica que tuvo su cuerpo en muchos años a consecuencia de la cual las gafas cayeron al suelo y se rompieron" (p. 121).[23] In effect, Benet utilizes a recurring form of metonymy. The *gafas oscuras*

---

[23]Mary's glasses are also mentioned on pages 117, 120, 211, 233.

take the place of the name, Mary. By the time of her death Mary *is* the black glasses in the mind of the reader and therefore, like many of the characters of the novel, becomes dehumanized. Other important symbols include the clock, which is a metonymic device substituted for time, Jorge's passion for biting ear lobes of the women with whom he has sexual intercourse, and the *fonda*, which is associated repeatedly with unfulfilled sexual desire and solitude. Due to the recurring appearance of these and other symbols the reader is able to make associations between themes and actions which otherwise could not be made. The symbols acquire specific meanings (as discussed above) and thereby facilitate the development of certain aspects of the novel (e.g., sex, time) which Benet desires to stress.

Although the images in *Una meditación* are generally concrete and precise, there exists in the novel an underlying mistrust of the ability of language to express accurately the narrator's intentions. This lack of confidence in language surfaces twice, and the narrator's concern with the problem serves both as a commentary by Benet on the writing of his own novel and as an explanation (or justification) of his peripatetic style. Appropriately enough, the subject of language appears in one of the narrator's digressions. When attempting to stir his memory into action, the narrator suddenly reflects upon his inability to describe his feelings: "No existe un verbo que defina la acción de fluir en el tiempo al conjuro de esos momentos que se arremolinan y encrespan... en los resquicios de un alma que se retrae apenas vislumbra con exacta y comprometedora certeza la sombra de una pasión que se cierne sobre sus nódulos sensibles..." (p. 137). Later the narrator adds that, "Tampoco existe ese otro verbo que defina la espera de un cuerpo, sumido en el deseo, que anhela a otro sin confiar nada a la esperanza" (p. 138). That is, the complexity of the narrator's mental processes cannot be described by the use of a simple verb or phrase. Only by expanding language to its maximum potential can the narrator effectively say what he wants to say. His narrative style, therefore, must necessarily be lengthy, complex and circumlocutory. In *Una meditación* it is abundantly clear that Benet agrees with his narrator, as the entire novel constitutes a reification of this point of view.

Una meditación forms the second part of Benet's trilogy on the ruination of the mythical Región. The destructive spatial environment of the novel, coupled with the fatalistic pessimism of the characters in their search for fulfillment, combine to form a novelistic reality similar to that of *Volverás a Región*. *Una meditación*, however, represents a more ambitious endeavor than Benet's first novel both in its intellectual suppositions and narrative technique. In his novel Benet does not simply reproduce individual thought processes and make them the basis of a flow of unconnected episodes. Behind the studied incoherence of the story Benet carefully weighs one element of the narrative against another, juxtaposing incidents for effect, engineering his structures as part of an overall plan. The guidance of a controlling intelligence makes itself felt in the ordering of the memories and frequently in the philosophical digressions to which they lead. Therefore, although the composite fragments of the past are presented in all the apparent confusion of their significance to the narrator, they are linked by an intellectual and artistic undercurrent.

Although the themes of sex and sexual desire recur throughout *Una meditación*, the novel is by no means erotic. The dehumanized, abstract nature of the characters, combined with the philosophical essence of the discussions on sex, tend ultimately to reduce the theme to a kind of impenetrable abstruseness. What remains palpable, however, is the constant desire of the characters to gain fulfillment through the satisfaction of their instinctual sex drives. Yet all the characters are doomed to failure. Benet reaffirms the Freudian principle that happiness is derived not merely from the discharge of psychic (i.e., sexual) energy, but through the establishment of lasting erotic relationships based upon love and affection.

In addition to the intellectual difficulties caused by the narrator's digressions on time, sex, memory, ruin, etc., the stylistic nature of *Una meditación* also imposes a formidable barrier to the comprehension of the novel. The series of parentheses, parentheses within parentheses, hyphens, subordinate clauses and the complex system of images all contribute to the creation of a style which is reminiscent of Faulkner's *Absalom, Absalom*. As one critic notes: "Es preciso volver continuamente sobre lo ya leído. Renuncio a citar un solo ejemplo, pues la cita me saldría

100

kilométrica. La novela está escrita de un tirón, aunque no se lea de un tirón; es decir, constituye un bloque compacto de tipografía opuesto al lector como una muralla."[24] However, the above critic errs in his implicit assumption that the stylistic wall which Benet constructs between the reader and the content of the novel must be totally destroyed. In fact, Benet seems deliberately (like Faulkner) to place obstacles in the path of the reader which prevent total comprehension. By means of his complex style Benet invents a reality which is more obscure and enigmatic than the realities external to his novel. He refuses to remove the obstacles which, once eliminated, would clarify the mysteries of his work. The events of *Una meditación* are maintained in a constant flux, and therefore many aspects of the novel remain paradoxical and intentionally insoluble.

[24]"*Una meditación* de Juan Benet," in *Literatura de España día a día: 1970-1971*, p. 226.

UNA TUMBA

Una tumba (1971) represents a significant departure from Juan Benet's first two novels in terms of style and narrative technique. It is by far the most easily understood and least complex of any of Benet's novels written to date. In contrast to the peripatetic narration of *Volverás a Región* and *Una meditación*, in which the concern with plot and dramatic development is only of secondary importance, *Una tumba* suggests Benet's preoccupation with a more traditional novelistic structure and plot formation. The novel is divided into four chapters, with the two middle chapters consisting of flashback scenes which help to clarify the denouement and explain the mysterious destiny of the child-protagonist.

Una tumba can best be classified as a short novel (as opposed to a long short story), and forms part of the series "Palabra e Imagen" published by Editorial Lumen. This series, which Joaquín Marco has described as "una selecta y valiosa colección minoritaria, donde la narración alterna con la poesía, donde la imagen contrapuntea al texto,"[1] includes such works as *Los cachorros* by Mario Vargas Llosa, *La ciudad de las columnas* by Alejo Carpentier, *Los días iluminados* by Alfonso Grosso and Camilo José Cela's *Toreo de salón e Izas, rabizas y colipoterras*. As the title "Palabra e Imagen" suggests, the books of this collection consist of both the written word and visual images in the form of photographs. Furthermore, the paper used in each selection varies in color, and is always of the highest quality. In *Una tumba* the paper is rosy pink with large dark pink type, the result of which produces a sharp contrast with the black and white photographs of the mansion which are interpolated throughout the novel. This elaborate composition, of course, is intended specifically to create a total esthetic experience for the reader. The book becomes, in Joaquín Marco's words, "un bello objeto":[2] the pho-

---

[1]Joaquín Marco, *Nueva literatura en España y América* (Barcelona: Editorial Lumen, 1972), p. 153.

[2]Joaquín Marco, p. 153.

tographs, the attractive cover, the colorful paper and print are designed to form an integral part of the novel *qua* artistic object. The plot of *Una tumba* appears uncomplicated when compared to the fragmented and incomplete stories of Benet's previous two novels. At the outset of the Civil War a "niño" (whose name we are never told), is left with an elderly couple charged with overseeing a mansion which the child will apparently inherit one day. During the course of the novel the niño fulfills a mysterious destiny in which he gains a kind of diabolical power from both his ancestors (whom we learn about through retrospective action) and the mansion he is to inherit. However, it is the ambience of the novel, and not the plot, which creates the primary interest and establishes the main tensions. As in his previous two novels, Benet carefully constructs the psychological and physical environment and creates a symbiotic relationship between his characters and their surroundings.

The Psychological and Physical Setting

By setting the action of *Una tumba* within the vicinity of Región, Benet immediately suggests the type of intestinal decay and ruin of the spatial background. The main action of the novel takes place in and around an abandoned mansion which, although not described verbally, is portrayed in a state of complete decadence by means of the photographs. These visual images paint a detailed portrait of the ruined house and the discarded objects within it, and serve as a vivid reification of the decadent physical environment which pervades the novel.

The most expressive symbol of both the physical and psychological environment is denoted in the title of the novel: "una tumba." As the novel begins the tomb lies in a state of negligent decay after remaining open for nearly two years. During the rainy months the grave becomes "una charca sucia y un criadero de mosquitos en la estación cálida."[3] Before the caretaker cleans

[3]Juan Benet, *Una tumba* (Barcelona: Editorial Lumen, 1971), p. 7. Future references to *Una tumba* will be taken from this edition and denoted in the text within parentheses.

it, the tomb is filled with "agua estancada... de color chocolate verdoso, circundada por una orla de baba negra y salpicada de cadáveres de insectos y hojas podridas y tallos flotantes envueltos en una minúscula pero tensa telilla pelágica" (p. 9). However, although the physical setting of the tomb clearly constitutes an integral part of the work, the psychological environment, based upon phantasmagorical appearances and ethereal descriptions, forms the nucleus of the novel. Benet creates his characteristically mysterious atmosphere in two significant ways: 1) by the use of magical realistic elements; 2) by suggesting realities which border on the edge of the fantastic, but which remain within the realm of superstition and fear.[4]

Benet forges the mysterious atmosphere of *Una tumba* from the outset. When the caretaker and the niño return from the grave after having spent the afternoon cleaning and draining it, the old man senses the mysterious presence of something he cannot actually touch: "[el guarda] sintió, si no la presencia a hurtadillas que se ocultó más allá de la luz rozando las sutiles aristas del vacío, al menos aquella otra clase de corpóreo soplo que agitó --perdiéndose-- las tinieblas más próximas de una noche escabrosa y fría" (p. 11). Benet's use of the oxymoronic "corpóreo soplo" further enhances the effect of the description: the paradoxical quality of the image suggests the elusive nature of what the old man feels. Even the motivation of the caretaker for cleaning the tomb remains nebulous: "El guarda parecía hacerlo de mala gana, como si hubiera recibido un mandato llegado desde muy lejos que le era imposible impugnar, desoir o discutir" (p. 11). The remains within the tomb itself are described as "malditos y temidos" (p. 31), the reason for which is revealed only later when the narrator relates the death of the Brigadier who is buried there. The mansion also possesses a silent power which arouses the fear

[4]My distinction here between magical realism and the purely "mysterious" elements is based upon my understanding of Luis Leal's discussion of *realismo mágico*, "El realismo mágico en la literatura hispanoamericana." Many of the enigmatic elements of the novel involve a purely mental fear or apprehension by a character that something preternatural is about to happen, or that there is a strange feeling in the air. This is distinct from magical realism, primarily because nothing supernatural has occurred or is in the process of occurring, and therefore the mysterious atmosphere is primarily a result of psychic anxieties.

of the characters. When the niño wanders through the rooms of the house he senses the ethereal forces at work on him: "Pero a medida que iba pasando de una habitación a otra... se iba familiarizando con las tinieblas y las sombras y con el adusto continente de todos los muebles y rincones.... Y tantas veces como se sentía llamado --la voz no sonora siempre más allá de la penumbra, el aliento de su propio yo en el ambiguo medio que clamaba por la devolución de su criatura de carne exilada en la tierra irredenta-- le era preciso detenerse para atender su creciente zozobra" (p. 86). Thus by the suggestive powers of his language Benet creates a psychological atmosphere of mystery, fear and superstition.

As we discussed in our earlier study of *Volverás a Región*, magical realism includes those incidents which do not have a logical or psychological explanation. In *Una tumba* Benet exploits this technique to the fullest extent and creates a magical atmosphere in some ways similar to that of Juan Rulfo's Comala. In the first place, Benet utilizes the mysterious voices of the dead to communicate with the living. The niño, whose destiny is inextricably linked to the voices of his deceased relatives, hears the murmuring and feels the presence of his ancestors. The Brigadier (great grandfather of the niño) makes his presence more tangible by entering the bedroom of the niño one evening while the child is speaking with his uncle. Inexplicably, the door to the room is suddenly thrust open, and the uncle senses the presence of the phantasmagorical Brigadier: "...entonces su tío se abalanzó de nuevo contra la puerta, maldiciéndole: maldito, vete de aquí, tú no tienes nada que decirle, maldito, maldito" (p. 91). Ultimately, the boy's father comes to the rescue of the uncle and saves him from the Brigadier's wrath: "Y ya no pugnaba [el tío] por cerrarla sino --sus manos magnetizadas en el picaporte-- por zafarse de su intolerable presión, cuando acudió su padre y a una orden suya no colérica pero sí dominante, consciente del poder que ejercía sobre todo el ignorado dominio, la hoja quedó libre e inerte, soportando en el picaporte el peso del caído sujeto a él todavía con sus dos manos..." (p. 92).

The third chapter of *Una tumba* is dedicated exclusively to portraying the Bridgadier's death, which occurred sometime during the early 1880's. Both the description of the Brigadier's murder and the effect on the lives of two of the participants clearly reflect an attitude of magical realism on the part of Benet. For reasons not totally explained, but which take root in the Brigadier's power and exploitation of the poor, the people of the vicinity conspire to murder the military officer during the celebration of a baby's baptism. During the dinner the Brigadier's food is poisoned "con cien gramos de cianuro potásico, una dosis suficiente para terminar con una punta de ganado" (p. 62). Realizing that the poison has had no effect, the conspirators add another dose to the Brigadier's dessert, which causes him to feel nauseated and retire to the water closet of the house, where he induces vomiting and soon returns to the table. After a few moments, however, he is overcome by a sudden pain and collapses, whereupon he is immediately taken to a nearby room. The doctor who treats the Brigadier is also involved in the murder plot, and instead of administering medicine, gives him another strong dose of poison. By some inexplicable power, the Brigadier still avoids death and soon realizes that he is being victimized by the persons attending the baptism. With a great surge of anger he escapes from the house by killing one of his guards and terrifying the others with a pistol. After recovering from their fright, the conspirators pursue the Brigadier with the aid of tracking dogs and finally discover him hidden in a small grove of trees. At this point "se abalanzaron sobre él, echando primero los perros, para acabar con su vida a puñaladas y culatazos. Incluso le dispararon a bocajarro dos disparos al pecho. A la vista de los sucesos decidieron deshacerse del cadáver y aquella misma noche lo arrojaron a un pozo de unos cincuenta pies de profundidad, situado en la misma propiedad y no lejos del lugar donde quisieron rematarle" (p. 67).

The following morning the murderers return to cover the well, only to discover that once again the Brigadier has escaped. Taking up the chase a second time, the men find the Brigadier, who now has lost all appearance of being human:

> ...su ropa era un amasijo de harapos húmedos, con numerosos agujeros por los que asomaba una carne blanca y señalada con moratones; casi no tenía cara, embadurnada de cieno negro manchado de sangre seca y una guirnalda de hojas podridas en torno a su

cuerpo; más que un hombre se hubiera dicho una especie de arcaico, desmesurado e indefenso molusco, que carente de caparazón ha de proteger su casi informe naturaleza con cuantos restos le oculten de los depredadores y bajo cuyo pusilánime y torpe aspecto, late una pugnaz y no descontenta sangre... (pp. 68, 73)

Finally the conspirators kill the Brigadier as "ocho fusiles o escopetas disparaban a la vez con los cañones apuntados hacia el suelo y a dos palmos del pecho en que abrieron un boquete del tamaño de una gatera" (p. 73). The Brigadier is buried and later exhumed by his son and placed in the tomb near the mansion.

I have described the Brigadier's death in such detail because I believe Benet based his description of the Brigadier on the personality of Rasputin, the diabolical Russian priest.[5] Like the Russian, the Brigadier is noted for his sexual prowess: "...para muchos [el Brigadier] gozaba de ciertos poderes demoníacos, el menor de los cuales no era, sin duda, su capacidad para conjurar la esterilidad" (p. 77). In addition, the Brigadier is regarded as "maldito" by his enemies and "sagrado" by his friends, in the same way as Rasputin was viewed in Russia. According to R. J. Minney,[6] Rasputin was murdered by a group of conspirators, but managed almost supernaturally to resist his death. The conspirators first attempted to poison Rasputin by putting enough cyanide in his food to kill him within seconds. When this failed --after eating the food Rasputin seemed to be totally unaffected-- they gave him a glass of wine with an equally large dosage of poison. When this also proved to be insufficient, the conspirators became somewhat terrified. Finally one of them lured Rasputin to a cabinet, and while the priest was staring through the glass, he was shot in the back in the area of the heart. One of the conspirators, a doctor, examined Rasputin and pronounced him dead. Meanwhile, as the murderers were making preparations to remove the body, Rasputin slowly began to move his eyelids,

---

[5] I have since spoken with Benet in Madrid and he has confirmed my contention that the Brigadier's character is patterned after that of Rasputin.

[6] R. J. Minney, *Rasputin* (New York: David McKay Co., 1973), pp. 188-203.

and suddenly reached out and tore the epaulette from the shoulder of one of the murderers. In a few moments, Rasputin gained enough strength to escape from the house and flee across the lawn, where he was once again shot, this time in the head and shoulders, and then beaten to death with a rubber club. Finally, the murderers hurled his body into a frozen river and hoped to be done with him forever. Strangely enough, an autopsy revealed that he died from drowning, thus proving that he was still alive when thrown into the water.

The Brigadier's death parallels so closely the death of Rasputin that Benet was obviously fascinated with the legendary Russian. Although several versions of Rasputin's death have gained popular appeal, Benet's use of the priest's diabolical personality and the inexplicable circumstances of his death clearly fit within the mysterious ambience of *Una tumba*.[7]

The realistic description of the Brigadier's reaction to his plight, combined with the detailed account of his grotesque death, form a direct contrast to the more than obvious inverisimilitude of the circumstances. Clearly, the Brigadier would "realistically" be unable to survive the enormous amount of poison and the gunshot wounds. There is no psychological or logical explanation for the Brigadier's ability to withstand the murder attempts, thus his death lies within the realm of magical realism. Even more inexplicable, however, are the deaths of the priest (who conspired against the Brigadier) and the child whose baptism furnished the favorable circumstances for the Brigadier's assassination.

The priest dies suddenly and mysteriously while celebrating mass: "...no bien hubo consagrado... se desplomó a los pies del altar derramando el vino sagrado sobre el ara y, con un rugido infrahumano, se abatió de bruces y agarrándose el vientre y dando volteretas quedó exánime en el refectorio 'despidiendo el espíritu con la sangre' que salió de su boca en forma de un único borbotón negro y humeante, denso y pestilencial como la colada de alqui-

---

[7]I realize that my digression on Rasputin is somewhat inconsistent with the overall methodology of my study. However, I believe that the digression is justified because it helps to explain the character of the Brigadier, who plays an important part in the intrinsic reality of the novel.

trán" (p. 78). The young child, on the other hand, experiences great pain and suffering due to "un violento sarpullido de granos de cabeza negra que en pocos días dejaron su cuerpo convertido en una pústula, un par de ojos abiertos a los que ya ni siquiera alcanzaba el dolor, viciados en el hedor de sus llagas y atentos tan sólo a la mueca macabra y sonriente de una boca inmóvil que cada día se agrandaba un poco más para mostrar sus blancas encías" (p. 79). In effect, the Brigadier has avenged his own death by causing the death of two persons associated either directly or indirectly with the conspiracy. The ubiquity of the Brigadier is especially mystifying: his spirit wanders through the area inspiring fear in the local inhabitants. Only during the two-year period when his tomb is ransacked and left open "[con] sus restos desperdigados y perdidos, dejó de sentirse su obstinada y malévola influencia" (p. 80).

The "Niño" and Destiny

The pervading tone of mystery and fear in Una tumba is suggested both by the elements of magical realism and by the superstitious beliefs of the characters. However, there exists a cause and effect relationship between these two aspects of the environment through the process of symbiosis: the preternatural atmosphere penetrates the minds of the characters and exerts a direct influence in their lives. Such is the case with the caretaker, who senses the hostility of his surroundings and lives in perpetual fear of the Brigadier's spirit. In broader terms, the entire population of the area is affected by the legendary Brigadier and his mansion. For this reason the people both fear and hate the dead man and wish to destroy his mansion. It is the niño, however, whose destiny is most directly linked to the Brigadier's power and who senses most intimately a kinship with the past.

The predestined relationship between the niño and the Brigadier is revealed early in the novel on two separate occasions, both of which are related to the tomb. In the first instance, the niño is assisting the caretaker with the cleaning of the tomb when suddenly "el sol brilló como no lo había hecho en muchos meses y la sombra del niño fue proyectada, de los pies a la cabeza, todo a lo largo de la tumba, para fijar sobre aquella película impresionable la silueta que el dominio había elegido como seña de identificación y reconocimiento del depósito que le tenía reservado" (p. 9). The following day, the child returns to the tomb, where "su atención quedó sujeta y fascinada por sus propias huellas en el fondo de la fosa, solidificadas por el hielo sucio de color caramelo que recubría las medias lunas de sus tacones" (p. 17). By associating the niño with the tomb Benet augurs the destiny of the child. The tomb represents the sinister and supernatural quality of the Brigadier's character which the niño will eventually inherit. In fact, through the body of the niño the Brigadier's spirit will take revenge upon the inhabitants of the area, beginning with the caretaker.

The intimate relationship between the niño and the mansion also forms an integral part of the child's destiny. Similar to his reaction to the tomb, the niño senses mysterious forces at work within the house which continually attract him toward an uncertain, but predetermined future. This deeply-rooted affinity between the house and the child is signaled from the beginning of chapter two, when the señora explains to the niño that, "Todo esto será tuyo un día" (p. 37). As the novel progresses and it becomes more and more evident that the niño will acquire the diabolical powers associated with the house and the Brigadier, the affinity between child and mansion intensifies. When describing the niño's walk through the house the narrator tells us that "Su propia imagen... parecía adecuarse al decorado, absuelta de su propio yo y convertida incluso en otro objeto más, dispuesto allí por la misma mano que había ingeniado tal acumulación para ocultar los últimos vestigios del cuerpo del niño..." (p. 88). If, as the narrator implies, the niño becomes interfused with the house, then what awaits him within the mysterious building? The narrator furnishes the answer explicitly only near the end of the novel, when the child hears and senses the presence of his ancestors: "...vio a la señora merodeando en torno a su cama y acercándose a su cabecera para abrirle su pecho.... También en el fondo estaba su padre y más allá su bisabuelo; a los que ya no tenía que vislumbrar sino tan sólo ver, seguirlos y obedecerlos" (p. 105). Thus the child submits to the inexplicable powers of his ancestral legend and becomes part of the eternal mystery of destruction and despair embodied by the decaying mansion.

As in each of Benet's first two novels, one of the primary concerns of *Una tumba* is the portrayal of solitude. This theme, and the correlatives of despair and waiting, are presented most dramatically through the niño, who is left by his father at the beginning of the Civil War and is later abandoned by the señora.[8] Throughout the novel the child constantly awaits or actively searches for an escape from his loneliness by means of regressing to the happiness associated with parental love. This search is portrayed in two significant ways: 1) by recounting the niño's relationship with his father; 2) by the desires of the niño to return to the protective womb, symbolized by his involvement with the señora. In the first instance, the narrator implies that a tight bond existed between the niño and his father which has been broken by the departure of the latter from Región. However, the child still remembers the ability of his father to assuage his loneliness even when acting in anger. When the caretaker with whom he is living becomes enraged, the niño accepts the curses "con la supina y sumisa obediencia con que había recibido años atrás la mirada de advertencia paterna, una boca entreabierta que ofreciera a las alturas el fugaz y jubiloso agradecimiento por la mano que, con negligencia y a su pesar tal vez, había descendido sobre su cabeza para desterrar el instante de soledad" (p. 15). When younger and still living with his father there existed a tacit agreement "entre padre e hijo, en virtud del cual el primero se comprometía a venir en ayuda del segundo siempre..." (p. 97). Thus the solitude of the niño, which was alleviated by paternal love and protection during previous years, becomes palpable once again in his life with the caretaker.

The niño's need to escape his solitude is most readily perceived in his relationship with the señora. What begins as an innocent concern by the woman for the protection of the child, grows into a type of deviant sexual intimacy which satisfies the desires of both persons. For the niño, the relationship represents a maternal love and desire to return to the womb. When lying

---

[8]The señora leaves the child in much the same manner in which "el niño con las gafas" is abandoned by his mother in *Volverás a Región*.

asleep beside the señora for the first time, he is suddenly
awakened by her breath on his cheek, and he moves nearer and
kisses her. What the child needs and desires is the maternal
protection offered by the woman's warm body: "...el niño volvió
a su posición en la almohada, fingiendo dormir, al tiempo que en
las sombras y en torno a él se cernía la presencia protectora que
sólo era capaz de percibir cuando no se sentía desamparado, un
envoltorio de algodón negruzco y cálido, prefigurando la aurora
paterna..." (p. 38). Even when their relationship advances to the
stage of sleeping naked together, caressing each other in the
dark, the niño is primarily concerned not with sexual arouse-
ment, but with escaping his solitude. When he gently presses his
fingernails into the señora's skin and traces a path over her
body, "...su carne insomne había anticipado toda la respuesta
que podía dar al enigma de una soledad cerrada al tiempo que los
surcos eran abiertos por sus dedos..." (p. 51). Thus the niño
continually attempts to liberate himself from the loneliness that
envelops him.

Paradoxically, the niño's final escape from solitude implies a
complete surrender to the solitude embodied by his ancestors
and the decaying mansion. When the child fulfills his destiny at
the end of the novel, he escapes the immediate loneliness only to
unite with the señora, his father and the Brigadier in an eternal
solitude: "Y de nuevo [el niño] volvió al dormitorio --flotando
sobre la losa hecha añicos-- en el centro de la casa de la que era
único poseedor... y, sobre todo, poseedor y dueño absoluto de su
soledad que ya no sería un atributo más del abandono sino la
manera de formar parte de todos aquellos que con tanta y tan
muda insistencia le habían reclamado..." (p. 106). Therefore,
although the niño becomes "dueño absoluto de su soledad," his
plight represents a type of mythical solitude, mitigated by its
mutuality, which takes root in the legend of the Brigadier and
gains tangible existence in the abandoned mansion.

Style and Technique

Una tumba is narrated from the perspective of a traditional,
third person omniscient narrator who relates the events and

penetrates the thoughts of the characters. In contrast both to *Volverás a Región* and *Una meditación*, *Una tumba* is written in a straightforward, direct manner of expression with almost a complete absence of marathon sentences or syntactical mazes. As Joaquín Marco wryly comments: "El relato que hoy nos ofrece Benet presenta una novedad con respecto al resto de su producción: resulta en conjunto mucho más comprensible..."[9]

Despite the dissimilarities, however, *Una tumba* shares certain stylistic traits with Benet's first two novels. For example, Benet's predilection for oxymoronic descriptions reappears in *Una tumba* and enhances the mysterious atmosphere of the novel. The "corpóreo soplo" (p. 11) of the wind intensifies the fear of the caretaker. The Brigadier's tomb is describes as "sagrado y maldito, venerado y exacrable" (p. 8), thus the legend of the Brigadier becomes even more disconcerting. When the Brigadier descends the steps of the house in order to escape his murderers, we hear the "eco sordo del peldaño" (p. 66). Taken as a whole, this recurrent use of oxymoron represents a stylistic trait which aids Benet in the creation of a mysterious novelistic reality based upon irresolution, antitheses and paradox.

Benet also utilizes various technical and stylistic elements in order to dehumanize his characters. In *Una meditación*, for example, he attributes animalistic traits to certain characters. His most frequent method of dehumanizing, however, involves the creation of abstract, ethereal characters by the suggestive powers of his style. In *Una tumba*, only the caretaker's wife is given a name (Mary), while the other characters are designated either by their age and sex or their profession: el niño, el tío, el padre, el guarda, el oficial, la señora, el Brigadier, el abuelo. In effect, Benet denies his characters humanizing features and reduces them to abstractions. Consequently, a majority of the characters symbolize concepts or ideas: niño-solitude; Brigadier-power, vengeance; señora-maternal love; guarda-fear; father-protection.

The concept of time is also an important element in *Una tumba*, and is directly affected by Benet's style of writing. The precise time span of the events of the novel remains unclear, primar-

[9]Joaquín Marco, p. 153.

ily because Benet consistently makes temporal references with deliberate ambiguity, even during the retrospective action of chapters II and III. For example, during the Civil War the tomb "había permanecido abierta casi un año, ó quizá dos" (p. 7). The niño's grandfather died "dos o tres años antes de la guerra" (p. 29), while his great grandfather (the Brigadier) was murdered "allá por el año 84 del siglo pasado" (p. 56). Even the duration of the Civil War in Región, which is specified as two years several times in the novel, becomes vague when discussed in the context of the mysterious tomb: "Tan sólo aquel --o aquellos dos-- año de guerra que la tumba permaneció abierta..." (p. 80). Benet frequently seems reticent to specify the time, primarily, I believe, because it would undermine his overall purpose of suggesting realities (including temporal ones) rather than naming them directly and succinctly.

Una tumba forms a unique part of Benet's novelistic repertory by virtue of its contracted length, the supplementary use of photographs and, above all, due to its relative simplicity. Nonetheless, the novel possesses several characteristics found in both Volverás a Región and Una meditación: the historical background of the Civil War, the recurring themes of solitude and decay and the mysterious environment of Región are portrayed in varying degrees of intensity in each of these novels. Furthermore, although Una tumba is stylistically a much less complex work, it shares with the other two novels such features as baroque-like sentences, the dehumanization of the characters, the deliberate withholding of meaning and the suggestive, rather than the precise use of language to create the overall novelistic reality.

Una tumba also reflects a social perspective which, although not as explicit (nor important) as in the novels of social realism, nonetheless furnishes an insight into Benet's view of the circumstances surrounding the Civil War. Concerning the constantly changing political climate in Spain before the war, Benet satirically notes that the shape of the garden, "parecía haber cambiado al compás de los avatares políticos de la España contemporánea" (p. 8). In addition, Benet attacks a certain element of the Republican forces (much like he does in Volverás a Región) by aiming his critical eye at the proletariat. When describing the ransacking of the mansion by the peasants, Benet details the defacing and looting of the house, and the subsequent all-night drunken orgy by the participants. The following morning, however, the peasants seem to regret their actions: "Un par de jóvenes... saludó al guarda con una viva la revolución cuya intención era desmentida por su tono sombrío y apologético" (p. 32). What Benet is suggesting, of course, is that the peasants did not join the revolution because of a philosophical commitment, but because of the ephemeral euphoria of being able to take revenge against the local landowner. In this instance, the peasants rebel against the legendary Brigadier and the power and wealth made tangible by the house.

The physical and psychological atmosphere of *Una tumba* reflects Benet's most characteristic manner of writing. Enhanced by the use of magical realism and the portrayal of fear and superstition, a sensation of mystery and destruction pervades the novel. Within this ambience the niño-protagonist awaits the fulfillment of his destiny. Like the principal characters of both *Volverás a Región* and *Una meditación*, the child is overcome by a predetermined future, against which it is impossible to struggle. As the narrator notes in reference to the Brigadier (the niño's great grandfather): "Era la cuarta generación que sufría su enojo" (p. 56). That is, the destiny of the niño is foreordained by the "enojo" of the Brigadier.

Although *Una tumba* has not received the critical acclaim granted *Volverás a Región* and *Una meditación*, it nonetheless constitutes an important part of Benet's novelistic art. It reveals a certain willingness (or desire) on the part of Benet to participate in an esthetic endeavor quite distinct from that which is normally involved in the writing of a novel. The result, in Joaquín Marco's view, is "un relato excelente,"[10] a work which is relatively penetrable, yet which remains characteristically abstruse and deceptive.

---

[10]Joaquín Marco, p. 155.

UN VIAJE DE INVIERNO

The complex, dense style of writing which characterizes *Volverás a Región* and *Una meditación*, reappears in Benet's fourth novel, *Un viaje de invierno* (1972). Whereas *Una tumba* represents a significant departure in both style and technique from his first two novels, *Un viaje* signals a return to the more complicated, nearly impenetrable narrative which characterizes nearly all of Benet's works of prose fiction. Once again the reader is forced to penetrate a world which consists of marathon sentences, a complex framework of recurring images, an ambiguous temporal structure and an interrelated series of events which remains essentially unexplained in terms of motivation and ultimate resolution. Benet's manipulation of incidents and descriptions to create the rarefied illusion of reality, coupled with the suggestive powers of his ethereal images and overall style, combine to form a reality which is clearly distinct from the novels of post-war Spanish realism.

As José Domingo has pointed out, *Un viaje* represents Benet's maximum effort to eliminate plot as an integral part of the novel: "*Un viaje de invierno* debe destacarse como el máximo logro en su objetivo de conseguir la abolición de todo lo que no sea el propio fluir de su prosa. Lo más que se consigue averiguar después de su lectura es la presencia de dos personajes: la vieja señora [Demetria] que prepara una fiesta con la que celebrar el previsto regreso de su hija Coré, y el hombre [Arturo] que está a su servicio y cuya marcha se espera una vez que la reunión haya sido celebrada."[1] Indeed, the characters of *Un viaje*, which perhaps can be described more accurately as "apparitions," are never brought into clear focus, but instead remain obscured in a dense fog. As a result, Benet succeeds in creating a mysterious world of shadowy figures who approach a destiny which, although never explicitly defined, is suggested by the title of the novel: a win-

[1]José Domingo, "Otro camino: el de Juan Benet," *Insula*, Vol. 28, N° 312 (noviembre de 1972), 6.

116

ter's journey or, more precisely, a journey toward death.[2]
In addition to stylistic and thematic elements, which will be
discussed later in this chapter, *Un viaje* shares important temporal and spatial characteristics with Benet's earlier novels. In the
first place, the spatial backgound of *Un viaje* consists of the area
in and around Región, the mythical region which forms the setting for each of Benet's three previous novels. Although not described in detail, the oppressive, ruinous atmosphere of Región
appears in *Un viaje* as an important component of the physical
and psychological environment. For example, the countryside
which surrounds La Gándara (the name of Demetria's property),
"tenía algo indefiniblemente inquietante: como si estuviera incli-
nado, colgado del cielo y a causa de una negligencia tan fútil que
nunca sería ya corregida, desprovista para siempre de horizonta-
lidad; como si precipitadamente hubiera sido abandonado, sin
tiempo ni razón para que fuera enmendado aquel minúsculo
error."[3] Even more disturbing, however, is the sensation of loneliness aroused by the physical characteristics of the area: "Pero
sobre todo, el desierto del monte, la fuga de sus habitantes, la
sensación de olvido unida a la de abandono, exagerada por la in-
soportable e inmitigable compañía de las moscas" (p. 219).
Demetria's house at La Gándara is submerged deeply in the
mysterious atmosphere of Región. In order to reach the house
one must decipher a complex maze of roads and pathways in
order to finally "encontrar en aquel laberinto el camino más corto
hasta una casa que carente de luces, oculta por la noche y los muros en sombras de la terraza, se imponía en el lugar con imper-
ceptible y secreto poder ni siquiera develado por sus secuaces y
servidores" (p. 131). In addition to its powerful, yet enigmatic
presence, the house at La Gándara exists in a state of perpetual

---

[2]The title *Un viaje de invierno* is derived from a collection of 24 songs composed
by Franz Schubert and the poet Wilhelm Muller under the title *Die Winterreise*
(1827, 1828). The central character of these songs is a youth, disappointed in
love and disillusioned by life, who sees only death as the ultimate end of his winter's journey.

[3]Juan Benet, *Un viaje de invierno* (Barcelona: La Gaya Ciencia, 1973), pp. 217-
218. Future references from *Un viaje...* will be taken from this edition and
denoted in the text within parentheses.

decay, similar to Dr. Sebastián's residence in *Volverás a Región*: "Algo en la casa estaba cambiando constantemente sin transgredir los límites de la quietud, algo que parecía parapetarse tras el silencio, la inmovilidad y la estanqueidad de un tiempo acrónico para no revelar la no permanencia e infinitesimal descomposición de cuanto había en ella" (p. 82).

Although the temporal setting of the novel remains vague, the Civil War and the post-war period are mentioned several times as a symbol of the past ruin which continues to influence the lives of the characters. This is especially evident in the life of Demetria. Few travelers pass through the valley near her home, and those who do bring news only of the "amargas reflexiones sobre la miseria de la postguerra y premoniciones acerca del mal tiempo avecinante" (p. 134). The conflict itself does not play an active role in the novel, but the resultant destruction is everywhere manifest in a people whose soul "quedó enterrada en la década del 30" (p. 180). In *Un viaje*, therefore, as in Benet's first three novels, the destructive power of the Civil War continues to gnaw at the heart of Spain and results in a negation of the life force through which the characters strive for meaning and fulfillment.

The Fiesta

Although there is no plot in *Un viaje* in the traditional sense, most of the "action" revolves around the fiesta. Demetria holds the affair each year, ostensibly to honor the return of her daughter Coré, who annually spends six months away from Región. The novel begins with the writing and mailing of the invitations, and terminates with a description of the party, which always takes place near the end of March. However, any attempt to comprehend the complex reasons for holding the celebration or to untangle the temporal confusion which surrounds the event encounters almost intransigent opposition. In the first place, the ambiguity of the party is signaled from the outset of the novel with the writing of the invitations. Each year Demetria writes the letters in long hand, though she is never aware of how many she has written nor how many guests she has invited. In fact, she never discovers how many persons come to the party because she does not attend herself. Instead, she remains locked in her room: "No bajaba al salón y no habría respondido a las llamadas en el supuesto de que hubiera habido alguien tan insensato como para hacerlas; si es que había algún asistente" (p. 100). Yet if Demetria never attends the party, why does she spend such a great deal of time planning for it? Indeed, why does she hold the party each year and why do the guests return?

First of all, though the narrator informs us that the party is celebrated each year to honor the return of Coré, there are several more important reasons which provide the impetus. José Ortega has suggested that the fiesta signifies: "a) suspensión del rigor, la rutina; b) forma de hacer volver a su marido y combatir la soledad ocasionada con su marcha, superando igualmente la enemistad con la familia de los Amat; c) instrumento para ejercer su voluntad."[4] The first and last of Ortega's suggestions can be consolidated to form the principal theme of the novel: the exercise of the will (la voluntad) in order to escape a predestined solitude and despair. However, it must be noted that the anguish which Demetria and her guests suffer is not an existential anguish in the strictest sense. According to existentialist thought, despair (and anguish) "means that we limit ourselves to a reliance upon that which is in our wills, or within the sum of the probabilities which render our action feasible."[5] In Un viaje the characters do not possess an active will. In fact, the entire novel can be viewed as an attempt by the characters to provoke a debilitated will into action; to do something to break loose from the monotonous and destructive routine of their lives. For Demetria, the fiesta presents an opportunity to exercise "una voluntad que --desengañada y resignada en muchos otros respectos-- tal vez convocaba aquella fiesta con el único objeto de demostrarse a sí misma su soberanía" (pp. 14-15). For the guests, the party provides an ephemeral mitigation of their predestined loneliness and symbolizes, if only temporarily, their flight from the pain of daily living:

[4]José Ortega, "Estudios sobre la obra de Juan Benet," Cuadernos Hispanoamericanos, N° 284 (febrero de 1974), 229-258.

[5]Jean-Paul Sartre, "Existentialism," in Existentialism from Dostoevsky to Sartre, ed. Walter Kaufmann (Cleveland and New York: World Publishing Co., 1956), p. 298.

"No dirían... de dónde escapaban ni de quién o qué huían; qué había en su habitual manera de vivir que tanto les dolía, qué era lo que aborrecían de sus costumbres, qué les embargaba --sin llegar a representarlo-- como una quimera irrealizable; por qué les entristecía su edad y su momento y su época y qué veían para más adelante que sin poder referirse al inmediato o remoto pasado sin una cierta acrimonia, les empujaba a acudir allí --sin confesar a nadie el camino de llegada-- en pos de un cierto alivio" (p. 177). Despite the explanations provided by the narrator, the fiesta remains an enigmatic and mysterious event. Only near the end of the novel is there a description of the party, and this is shrouded in mystery and magic. The musician, whose destiny is interwoven with that of Arturo and Schubert's waltz, sits at the piano to play, but the keys begin to move before he touches them: "Pero no permitía [el piano] ser tocado porque anticipándose a los dedos las teclas descendían antes de ser oprimidas por las yemas..." (p. 238). Likewise, the pedal of the piano "es hundido a fondo antes de que el pie lo pisara" (p. 239). The unknown guests also add to the impalpable nature of the party. Do persons actually attend the fiesta, eat, drink and dance? The narrator implies that they do, not by describing their presence but rather by portraying the house after the party is over: "Las sillas caídas y algunos vasos por los suelos, ceniceros repletos de colillas, manchas de líquidos y desparramados frutos secos y unas cortinas abombadas por el céfiro de la mañana, delante de un ventenal que ha quedado descuidadamente abierto..." (p. 107). Furthermore, Benet suggests the psychological (and perhaps physical) nature of the guests by their state of non-being: "Todos ellos sabían de sobra que habían muerto, que ni siquiera necesitaban mencionarlo porque la mirada --el primer vistazo-- bastaba" (p. 235). Thus the magical movement of the piano, combined with the "unreal" atmosphere of both the house and the guests, creates a climate of magical realism similar to that of *Una tumba* and *Volverás a Región*, in which Benet searches for the mysterious elements of reality which defy logical and psychological explanation.

The Portrayal of Time

We are never aware in *Un viaje* of a pure present, nor is a specific past very often exclusively defined. In fact, Benet seems purposely to create a timeless vision of reality in which past and present are interfused to form a vague series of occurrences which defy order and reason. For example, although the fiesta is held each year near the end of March, Demetria is unable to formulate a chronological ordering of the peculiar nature of each party. Instead, the parties become shuffled and confused in her memory: "barajadas [las fiestas] entre sí daban lugar a cierta confusión entre las fechas y las singularidades de cada fiesta lo que, al menos, gozaba de la propiedad de romper la escala aritmética para establecer una cronología con otros cánones" (p. 21). Further temporal ambiguity in the novel is achieved by the narrator's frequent reluctance to specify the duration of a particular event or action. When describing the approach of the horse to La Gándara, the narrator remarks that, "No fue posible saber cuándo asomó por primera vez entre las encinas de La Loma, más allá del camino de pacientes. Bien podía haber sido un año atrás --o cinco--..." (p. 215). The musician's wait at La Gándara for the servant to open the door is described in equally vague terms: "No esperó mucho... o tal vez sí, un par de años, un par de segundos u horas o décadas" (p. 234). Also, when portraying Demetria's fear of altering the destiny of Amat, the narrator claims that, "Eso fue lo que la cegó, lo que la hizo obstinada durante dos días o dos semanas cruciales" (p. 118). Benet purposely develops his novel within a temporal structure which is rarely specified, and thus the ambiguity of time contributes to the overall elusiveness of the work.

As José Ortega notes in his study of *Un viaje*, the "journey" indicated in the titled suggests several possible movements: the return of Coré to La Gándara, the possible return of Amat, the annual journey of the guests to attend the party, Arturo's movement toward Mantua, Demetria's excursion into town to cancel the printed invitations after twelve years of living in isolation, the arrival of the *Intruso* or the itinerary of the musician.[6] The

[6]José Ortega, p. 250.

participants in all of these journeys share a common desire to comprehend a personal destiny which always remains beyond their reach. This becomes readily apparent when viewed in light of their relationship to the fiesta: the musician attends the party after failing at his profession in Central Europe, Coré and Amat are linked to the fiesta through Demetria, the invited guests are obviously associated with the party, Demetria travels to town to cancel printed invitations for the party, the *Intruso* appears at the party itself and Arturo becomes involved with the fiesta to such an extent that he begins to wonder whether it is being held in his honor. Therefore, given that all of these possible trips revolve around the fiesta, the key to understanding the theme of the novel lies within the journey to the event:

> En ese viaje anual, en la conmemoración de la vuelta de una muchacha que probablemente no vive y en la espera del castigo a un indisciplinado viajero que aún no se ha puesto en ruta ¿no existe el deseo de anular en un día todo el tiempo transcurrido en el ámbito social de las costumbres? Y esa reincidencia de todos ellos --tanto los de Región, como los de la otra vertiente de la montaña-- en una serie de actitudes y creencias no elaboradas ni cristalizadas en hábitos, ni inscritas en los anales ni presentes en el impasse de la memoria colectiva, ¿no esconderá el anhelo por ese acto único --ni repetible ni, paradójicamente, reversible-- que --no está la fecha en el calendario ni el lugar en el mapa, sublimados en el espacio-tiempo anterior a la historia-- les liberará por una noche del destino común? (p. 182)

In effect, these people undertake the journey in order to annul time, to exist in a temporal vacuum where neither past, present nor future possesses any reality. Once the concept of time is eliminated, the characters are able to escape a destiny which no longer exists.

However, as occurs in both *Volverás a Región* and *Una meditación*, the characters of *Un viaje* are trapped in the past and therefore have no potentialities for a meaningful future. If, as with Bergson (and Benet), life consists of a continuation of the past into an ever-growing and expanding present, then the characters of *Un viaje* can have no hope for the future, since their lives are composed of "un ayer envuelto en ámbar temporal sin movimientos ni enigmas, sin evolución ni crecimiento ni estaciones ni sonidos, en el epiceno limbo del ser-fue, situado más allá de la anespacial fisura señalada en el curso de la existencia por el divorcio entre voluntad de vivir y continuidad" (p. 103). Although the fiesta represents for the characters an opportunity to grasp "the silent strength of the possible,"[7] they remain ensnared by a stagnant present in which everything is past --"un pudo ser" (p. 154).

Although Benet portrays the characters by distinguishing between present and past, with the latter permeating the former, he completely obliterates time during the majority of the novel. Instead of using the time-shift technique, in which the temporal focus continually shifts, Benet presents a temporal vacuum in which the sense of duration becomes so rarefied that days and months lose their independent value, fuse and disperse into emptiness in which chronological time ceases to have meaning and therefore to exist. Like many novels of the twentieth century, *Un viaje* contains no recognizable system of time counting, and the final sentence of the novel seems to bleed into the first and gyrate indefinitely within the work itself.

Fatalism and Destiny

The fatalistic concept of destiny which is portrayed in each of Benet's first three novels reaches its fullest and most critical development in *Un viaje*. As he does in his other novels, Benet eliminates the dimension of free choice for his characters by infusing them with a fatidical acceptance of their destiny. Benet portrays the future of the characters in two complementary ways: 1) by the use of symbols and leitmotivs associated with the use of magical realism; 2) by portraying the conflict between a free, active *voluntad* versus a predetermined destiny.

According to most existential thinkers, existence precedes essence. That is, man (without God) exists in the world before he

---

[7]See note 14, chapter III.

can be defined by any conception of himself. In Sartre's terms: "...man first of all exists, encounters himself, surges up in the world --and defines himself afterwards.... Man is nothing else but that which he makes of himself."[8] Therefore, a person will never be able to explain the action of another by reference to a given and specific human nature. In other words, there is no determinism in existentialist philosophy: man is free to choose and act as he pleases, and must suffer if he chooses wrongly or unwisely. In *Un viaje*, Benet creates an anguish and despair as equally destructive as that of the existentialists, but he does so by eliminating choice. For Benet, like Faulkner and Proust before him, man is not condemned to be free, but rather is doomed before he makes a decision. This is clearly evident in *Un viaje* for both Arturo and Demetria, whose lives are guided by a continuous journey toward death.

Demetria's life is governed by a type of nineteenth-century positivism in which she cannot escape her *race* and *moment*. Early in the novel Benet asserts that she is inextricably bound to a solitary existence in Región because of her parentage: "...habiendo heredado de los padres innominados la obediencia a una ley que no se preguntaba (por falta de tiempo, tal vez, por exceso de trabajo) sobre sus fundamentos, habiendo afincado en las tierras bajas del Torce, había remontado su curso para oponer su mentis a una causalidad demasiado natural, demasiado lícita y por consiguiente --para la mentalidad cismática-- moralmente recusable" (p. 34). Although Demetria lives as a recluse in almost total isolation --"Hacía muchos años que vivía sola, reducida, inmersa y tan compenetrada con esa soledad que deja de ser un estado para convertirse en una condición" (p. 99)-- the source of her greatest anguish takes root in her inability to act in defiance of her circumstances: "No me pongo enferma cuando pienso en los años de soledad que todavía me aguardan.... Sí me duele, en cambio, mi impotencia y la poca capacidad de persuasión de la fantasía a la que, por más que quiero no logro convencer para que se haga dueña de la voluntad y arroje fuera de mí estas estériles costumbres que han anticipado mi muerte sobre la hora de mi fa-

---

[8]Sartre, cited in Kaufmann, pp. 290-291.

124

llecimiento" (p. 222).

Arturo's journey toward the source of the Río Torce in Mantua is portrayed from the beginning as an inevitable "viaje de invierno." Arturo knows very little about his past, except that for nearly all of his life he has labored on the farms along the Torce valley and has slowly journeyed up the river: "Toda su trayectoria parecía determinada por aquel lento, pero progresivo alejamiento de la ciudad, para remontar el curso del río y cambiar de casa y amo, mediante un salto de unos diez kilómetros cada seis u ocho años" (p. 26). His residency at Demetria's house is only temporary, since his final destiny lies beyond La Gándara in the forests of Mantua.

Arturo's gradual movement toward Mantua defies logical explanation: he is "impulsado por la secreta obediencia a la ley que le dictara remontar el curso del río" (p. 39). Similar to Dr. Sebastián of *Volverás a Región*, Arturo's destiny is determined by a number of elements from the "real" (albeit mysterious) world and the realm of magical realism. In the first place, Arturo's future was predetermined early in his youth when one evening he listened to a waltz (el vals K) in the music conservatory where his mother worked as a cleaning lady. In the same way that the telegraph wheel foretells and dictates the future of Dr. Sebastián, the waltz mysteriously guides Arturo toward Mantua: "[el vals] le enseñó en la ignorancia el único camino que había de seguir para buscar su destino en las tierras de Mantua" (p. 238).

Before he reaches Demetria's house, his final stop before arriving at Mantua, Arturo is granted a partial exercise of free will to determine the future. The decisions that he makes, however, are inexplicably related to the eternal cycle of nature: "En años sucesivos y siempre por las mismas fechas [su marcha] se había de repetir... para hacerle sentir como casi todas sus determinaciones concertaban con el estado de la naturaleza y, en un ignorado calendario sin duda preciso y secreto dentro de la ambigua e inútil rebelión del clima a la rígida disciplina de los ciclos, habían quedado fechados" (p. 42). The recurring symbol of the jackdaws (*grajos*), for example, can only be understood in terms of the birds' instinctual migratory habits during the warm and cold seasons of the year. The jackdaw is mentioned repeatedly in the novel,[9] and thus becomes a leitmotiv which indicates Arturo's own migration up the river. The flow of the river also becomes a symbol of Arturo's continual movement, as suggested in the Greek epigram (διά ρόον) at the beginning of the novel. In addition, Arturo's ultimate fortune, "el conocimiento de la muerte" (p. 90), is signaled by the allusion to Numa, the omnipotent guardian of the Mantuan forests. As we have discussed earlier in our study of *Volverás a Región*, Numa's existence is based upon the negation of logic and Benet's affinity for the magical and inexplicable. In *Un viaje*, Numa is mentioned several times, and is described with characteristic abstruseness: "...un hombre que dormía todo el año y solamente despertaba cuando sentía la tierra de sus señores hollada por pies extraños" (p. 178). Numa's presence in the novel is important, of course, because he serves as a distressing reification of the death which awaits Arturo at the end of his winter's journey. However, as occurs with nearly all of the enigmatic and magical elements in his novel (in this instance, the appearance of the jackdaws, the power of the waltz and the portrayal of Numa), Benet neither justifies nor explains their presence.

The destiny of the musician (who in typical Benetian fashion remains without a name), also forms an integral, though less important, part of the novel, and is linked directly to the lives of Demetria and Arturo. As youths, both the musician and Arturo visited the conservatory on the same evening, and both heard the waltz played on the piano. As discussed above, the music urges Arturo toward Mantua and his death. For the musician, however, it infuses him with an obsession to become a recognized master of the piano, while at the same time it denotes his ultimate failure. His realization of the latter becomes tangible during his trip to Austria (the country of the waltz), where a waiter in a café informs him of another colleague who years earlier had searched for a meaning and reason to his profession. The musician suddenly realizes that his search is in vain and returns to Región, where he continues to search for the mysteries of music

[9]The *grajo* appears on the following pages: 39, 46, 70, 72, 76, 79, 84, 100, 134, 157, 190, 204, 219, 224, 265.

(and life) by listening to his music box and playing the *organillo*. For her part, Demetria follows closely the career of the musician, but has realized from the beginning that he will never become a success (i.e., will never decipher the mystery of the waltz). Therefore, after his return from Austria she invites him to her annual fiesta, which he attends like the other guests in hope of exercising his will and discovering the answers for which he has been searching. He fails, of course, as indicated when the piano begins to play before he touches the keys, and by the gust of wind which scatters his musical scores throughout the room and into the yard. As the papers become strewn about, the musician pathetically grasps a lamp, "para a cuatro patas por todo el salón proseguir la búsqueda de las hojas manuscritas que había de prolongarse mientras agotada la voluntad gozara todavía de un último ápice de su propio sentido" (p. 241).

The destructive destiny of the characters of *Un viaje* --of Arturo, Demetria, the musician and the guests-- intensifies the atmosphere of paralytic despair and anguish which pervades the novel. However, as discussed earlier, the profound agony is not based upon existential doctrine, since Benet eliminates free choice for his characters by condemning them to a predetermined and always fatalistic future. As in his three previous novels, Benet juxtaposes the purely deterministic elements with aspects of magical realism, and thereby underscores his propensity for constructing realities which proceed from the mysterious and the inexplicable.

Style and Technique

As we discovered in our study of *La inspiración y el estilo*, Benet maintains that a writer's style is his principal instrument for creating his novelistic reality. Indeed, not only does the writer discover and subsequently portray the enigmas of reality, but he also invents reality through the skillful use of language. In *Un viaje*, Benet concentrates on creating an enigmatic environment for his characters based upon the suggestive powers of his style. He does not attempt, as do the post-war neorealists, to classify, categorize or name things directly. In fact, he explains very little. As a consequence of his style Benet succeeds in creating an uneasy and mysterious mood by suppressing information, and by portraying both persons and objects with ethereal, intangible images and stylistic devices.

A large part of Benet's style of writing in *Un viaje* seems to be based upon the desire to avoid translating sensation into perception. A cognitive knowledge of something, be it of a character, an object or a particular ambience, is of secondary importance to the awareness of a situation in terms of pure consciousness of it. In this sense, Benet can be viewed as an idealist: since our consciousness seizes nothing but manifestations, reality is very illusory. When reading *Un viaje*, we sense that we are before the dream of reality, instead of reality itself. Indeed, much of Benet's style supports this point of view.

Benet creates an illusory reality in *Un viaje* by presenting characters who do not really seem to exist. Demetria's daughter, Coré, for example, never appears in the novel and her actual existence is open to question. On the one hand, she exists because she has been registered with the official government offices: "...en todos los archivos y censos obraba el registro de Coré --Coré Amat-- e incluso debía existir en un juzgado una carpeta con el expediente cobijado bajo su nombre" (p. 191).[10] On the other hand, however, Benet suggests that Coré is not a physical being, but rather lives only in the mind of Demetria "como más hija de la fantasía que de la carne" (p. 189). Likewise, but to a greater degree, Demetria's husband Amat never appears as an actual human being, but instead exists as a manifestation of Demetria's nostalgic memory: "Fuera de sí misma no existía posiblemente la menor traza de Amat, ni de su existencia anterior ni de su hipotético paradero actual, ni de su paso por Región o por su casa ni, menos aún, de su legitimación como marido" (p. 191). Thus both Coré and Amat are portrayed through the consciousness of Demetria, and both characters remain within the shadowy dimension between existence and non-existence: "Amat o Coré, ambos eran personificaciones de un deseo extinguido en la memoria, complementarios uno de otro en cuanto a su transposición al te-

---

[10]Benet's reference to the government offices represents an obvious satire of a governmental bureaucracy in modern society.

rreno de los hechos recordados y registrados" (p. 191).
Although the existence of Demetria cannot seriously be
doubted, her description represents the most explicit example of
Benet's predilection for the intangible and the ethereal. In the
first place, the inhabitants of Región know Demetria by more
than one name: "Si en algunos lugares y épocas del año se le co-
nocía por Demetria, en otros en cambio lo era por Nemesia" (p.
102). In addition, Demetria is familiar to many people of Región
by her nickname "Obscura," the mysterious connotations of
which are more than obvious. Benet never ascribes physical
characteristics to Demetria, but when describing her voice,
hands or general appearance he consistently shrouds her in mystery and a state of non-being. Her sudden apparition in front of
Arturo, for example, is described as follows:

> ...[ella] apareció ante él despojada de tiempo y co-
> loreada por la nada, simple yuxtaposición de su figu-
> ra al instante incóloro tan sólo representado en el
> miedo: insomne y sin sombras, ni siquiera había en su
> cara el asomo de una carne viciada por la espera, áto-
> na y casi argentífera, desprovista de toda emoción:
> no había llegado hasta allí, no había estado observán-
> dole mientras acuclillado hurgaba en la grama sino
> que empezó a formarse con la llegada del repentino
> frío, para condensarse en su figura negra con el movi-
> miento de sus ojos hacia un cielo nacarado (y estriado
> en el horizonte) que señaló con el dedo. No estaba allí
> sino que él mismo la había llamado con su temor, re-
> ferido a aquel tiempo por el que --justamente enton-
> ces, ni antes ni después-- acababa de pasar. (pp. 92-
> 93)

Furthermore, Demetria possesses a "mano impalpable" (p. 81),
and when speaking she utters "palabras sin vocalización" (p.
97). Her voice is "concertada con el silencio y la oscuridad, sin
timbre ni tono" (p. 97), and when one evening she reaches out to
touch Arturo, the latter feels "un par de manos sin tacto" (p.
98). In order to stress further Demetria's non-being, the narrator
suggests that on occasion Arturo sees only the image of Demetria, not the woman herself: "Cuando la imagen de la señora
(probablemente no la señora misma)..." (p. 95). Thus Benet's

entire method of portraying Demetria supports his contention that we can sense only the image of something and not the thing itself. In this instance, Benet's avoidance of concrete and tangible images, coupled with the total absence of adjectives to describe Demetria's physical make-up, suggest her non-reality as a human being. However, despite Demetria's non-existence in the traditional sense, she suffers "real" anguish and "real" despair as she attempts to come to terms with her destiny.

Benet's predilection for relegating his characters to an ethereal type of existence does not extend to the rest of the atmosphere of *Un viaje*. As in each of his previous novels, Benet utilizes personification as a means of contrasting his characters with the environment in which they live. For example, Demetria's house is surrounded by an actively hostile nature which aspires to gain control of the area: "Una línea de aylagas, de geráneos, de dalias, de filipéndulas y prímulas contorneaba la fachada principal de la casa como para constituir un primer parapeto ante el acoso de una naturaleza que se había apoderado de toda la heredad..." (p. 33).[11] The violence of the winter months is also portrayed by means of personification. During the dark days of winter the black poplar trees are stripped of their leaves: "...el negro esqueleto de los chopos --desprovistos de toda carne en la radiografía hibernal [estaban] teñidos en la pudrición e instantáneamente detenidos en el momento de su desaparición" (pp. 57-58). In fact, the hostility and overwhelming might of the frigid months of Región banish the spirit of life from the area: "...se vio que hasta el espíritu del árbol había huido hacia los encinares del otro lado del Torce, un desordenado triángulo taciturno que diera en lamentar su exilio en el reino de la luz donde purgaba su perennidad ganada a costa de renunciar al afán de regeneración que, con la sangre menstruada y seca de los robles, con el manto damasceno de helechos y tobas, había marchado a refugiarse en las sombras para recoger nuevas fuerzas en la pudrición" (p. 58). Therefore, the essence of the ambience in *Un viaje* takes root in a two-fold presentation of reality. On the one hand we have a vigorous repre-

[11]From a different point of view, the flowers symbolize the temporary victory of man (reason) over the forces of nature.

sentation of a personified nature in which the images are palpable and boldly defined. On the other hand, the recurrent images which suggest the non-existence of the characters remind us of the illusory reality which appears in the novel as if in a dream. Benet's style of writing in *Un viaje* is similar to that of both *Volverás a Región* and *Una meditación*. In characteristic fashion he utilizes page-length sentences, complicated syntax, parentheses and parentheses within parentheses. However, Benet seems to exert a control over the flow of his prose in *Un viaje* which is absent from his previous full-length novels: he exercises restraint in the length of his sentences and paragraphs, and eliminates many of the subordinate clauses which characterize much of his earlier writing. In addition, he places many of his typical digressions in the margins of the page in reduced-size print instead of within the narrative itself. As a result, the more condensed nature of his prose appears less peripatetic than usual. Nonetheless, Benet's style continues to evolve as a complex webwork of language replete with delays and confusions. As Pedro Antonio Urbina notes: "La prosa de Benet ondula, se alarga, se retuerce, como bajo una tensión producida por un impulso para alcanzar las claves y la parsimonia de los meandros en los que se recrea el estilo."[12] Thus Benet's intricate style, although mitigated to some extent, maintains in *Un viaje* the fundamental traits which lead Ricardo Gullón to designate it as "un estilo laberíntico."

Symbols and Leitmotivs

Benet frequently utilizes recurring symbols and leitmotivs in his novels. In *Volverás a Región*, such symbols as the black car, the "camioneta" or the "moneda de oro" affect both the fragmentary nature of the narrative and the ambiguity of certain events of the plot. In *Una meditación*, the recurring appearance of the clock and the rats is used as an effective metonymic device to portray time and sex. In *Un viaje*, Benet once again utilizes a variety of symbols which recur throughout the work, the majori-

---

[12]Pedro Antonio Urbina, "Juan Benet, *Un viaje de invierno*," *Indice*, N° 310 (1 de julio de 1972), 25.

ty of which either enhance the mysterious atmosphere of the novel or affirm the ultimate destiny of the characters.

Most outright repetition in literature has two important purposes: 1) simply to make the reader remember something; 2) to intensify the meaning associated with the experience or object which is repeatedly described.[13] In *Un viaje* Benet utilizes both of these aspects of repetition by his development of several symbols. One of the most important of these is the *bausán*, a small straw doll which Demetria keeps on the nightstand near her bed. As José Ortega has suggested, Demetria's concerted effort to erase the past and combat her involuntary memory takes concrete form in the *bausán*,[14] an object which is directly linked to Amat (Demetria's husband), who fled La Gándara and Demetria on the evening of the first fiesta. The *bausán*, which reappears throughout the novel,[15] enables the abandoned woman to endure her solitude and displace her sexual frustration. In addition, the doll plays an important role in the relationship between Demetria and Arturo. Since Demetria invariably hides the doll from Arturo's view (an act which symbolizes her mysterious control over the servant), the final journey of Arturo is signaled by the object's permanent disposal: when Demetria locks the doll in the closet, she realizes her permanent emptiness and solitude and the inevitable journey of Arturo toward Mantua: "Cerró con llave el compartimento donde guardaba el bausán. Sabía que no le volvería a ver, que al día siguiente --sin que entre ellos mediara una palabra-- quedaría resuelto el contrato, con una muesca vertical sobre las runas inclinadas y horizontales de la jamba, con su esperada pero intempestiva marcha hacia los confines de Mantua. Que tal vez eso significara el final de muchas otras cosas, incluida la tradición del festejo y toda aquella larga serie de transgresiones a la ley de espera, transferidas al bausán desde la memoria de Amat" (p. 232).

[13]For an in-depth study of repetition in literature and film, see Bruce Kawin's *Telling It Again and Again* (Ithaca and London: Cornell University Press, 1972).

[14]José Ortega, p. 253.

[15]The *bausán* appears on the following pages: 13, 35, 50, 54, 66, 67, 86, 128, 164, 204, 205, 207, 212, 213, 232.

Benet also utilizes an interrelated group of recurring symbols which includes the loss of electrical power (*avería*), the night light in Demetria's room and the lantern which the musician carries as he approaches La Gándara to attend the fiesta. The temporary loss of electrical power, which coincides with Arturo's arrival at La Gándara, signals the beginning of winter and intensifies the mystery which surrounds the two main characters. The second loss of electricity (which occurs at an unspecified time) bears even more significance because it provides the key to understanding the meaning of the lantern and the night light. When the lights go out for the second time, Demetria advises Arturo --in a mysterious atmosphere of shadows and the waning light of a match-- not to attempt to light anything: "...se hicieron audibles las palabras... 'No alumbres nada,' de unas tinieblas sin tráquea --extinguidas al mismo tiempo que la llama pero tan perceptibles por su estela asonora--..." (p. 97). Later the same evening when Arturo is resting in bed, he hears the same voice emanating from the darkness: "A tientas buscó la caja de fósforos y encendió uno, no para desterrar las tinieblas sino para hacer audibles pero no sonoras --durante el plazo exacto en que permaneció encendido-- las mismas palabras inconfundibles que le ordenaran o le advirtieran (careciendo de tono tanto podían ser imperativas como admonitorias) no alumbrar nunca nada" (p. 98). In effect, Demetria's words imply that any attempt by Arturo to clarify the mystery of his destiny will result only in failure. Demetria's own unsuccessful search for an explanation to her solitude is symbolized by the night light (pp. 52, 97, 160, 163, 221, etc.) which she keeps in her bedroom. Likewise, the musician's desire to understand the mysteries of his life is symbolized by the lantern which he carries on the path to La Gándara (pp. 52, 132, 157, 169, etc.). The relationship between the night light and the lantern --and between Demetria and the musician-- is indicated early in the novel before we are aware of the musician's existence: "[Arturo] quedó sorprendido por el parpadeo de la mariposa en su ventana (prefiguración de las vacilaciones de la linterna del maestro, en su ascensión a la casa)..." (p. 52). Thus the recurring symbols of the short circuit, lantern and night light combine to enhance the enigmatic nature of the characters' lives and underscore the impossibility of finding a solution to their agony and despair.

The conflict between reason and instinct, which forms an integral part of both *Volverás a Región* and *Una meditación*, reappears with less intensity in *Un viaje*, and is linked to the theme of *voluntad*. In his earlier novels Benet repeatedly affirms that, although instinct is the predominant force in man's life, reason exerts the most important influence in civilized society. In *Un viaje* this conflict is portrayed by the symbol of the horse and its instinctual movement toward Demetria's house.[16] Characteristically, there is no logical explanation for the existence of the horse. He first appears --the narrator tells us that perhaps he appears-- when Arturo decides to accept a position in the home of Demetria: "Es posible que por aquel entonces, en una pradera del otro lado del río, pastara un caballo con las manos atadas con una soga. Pero sólo es posible" (p. 41). As the novel develops the horse first comes into view quite far from La Gándara, but slowly descends toward the house: "Poco a poco el caballo se había ido acercando, sin movimientos perceptibles, a la cerca de la finca, descendiendo desde el punto más alto del encinar donde apareciera días antes, hacia la vaguada que la separaba de la dehesa vecina" (p. 162). The actual movement of the horse parallels that of the guests who attend Demetria's party. Liberated from the oppressive influence of reason, and incited by an instinctual need to escape their common destiny of loneliness and suffering, the guests undertake their annual journey to La Gándara. As the narrator remarks concerning the horse, but which can be applied with equal accuracy to the guests: "Todo el tiempo... sentía la misma inquietante compulsión (afín al milagro) que pugnaba por zafarse de la opresión en el pecho en busca de aquella liberación... que tal vez (sin poder sustraerse a ella) acarrearía su propia destrucción (o al menos eso es lo que desde muy lejos se dijeron para sí los grajos, cuando al traspasar la cerca remontaron su vuelo" (p. 219). Referring specifically to the journey of the guests, the narrator asks rhetorically: "¿No pone de manifiesto que es común a todos el deseo de ponerse por un día a resguardo de la ra-

---

[16]The symbol of the horse appears on the following pages: 41, 58, 59, 160, 162, 169, 207, 215-221, 241.

134

zón?" (p. 182). However, as occurs with nearly all of Benet's characters, the possibility of escape soon becomes transformed into the inevitability of failure. Neither the guests nor the horse will complete their journey. As the narrator asserts concerning the horse: "toda su vida era una equivocación, había seguido durante tanto tiempo y tan inconscientemente un trayecto erróneo que cuando se apercibió de ello --siempre un ayer inmediato-- ya estaba demasiado lejos para reunirse con un mundo en orden. No llegaría nunca" (p. 220).

Two of the most enigmatic symbols of *Un viaje* are the *Intruso*, who appears at the fiesta as well as at the Conservatory, and the *bufanda*, which the Intruder leaves at Demetria's house each year at the end of the fiesta. The scarf "no sería reclamada porque carecía de poseedor" (p. 19). The act of abandoning the scarf suggests a kind of nostalgic desire to reclaim the past. Demetria, of course, continually resists this urge, since she aspires to situate herself within a temporal vacuum in which neither past nor future exists. As José Ortega aptly notes: "La bufanda introduce la finalidad, pues alguien ha de venir a recogerla, pero es sólo el azar, manteniendo despierto al ánimo en continua espera, el que posibilita la incierta vuelta del Intruso."[17] For his part, the Intruder represents the deceptive promise of both the guests, who hope to avoid their destiny, and the musician, who desires to become an accomplished professional. Although the origin and identity of the Intruder remain unknown --"se barajarían las hipótesis más dispares acerca de su procedencia y de su personalidad" (p. 109)-- the narrator implies that his attendance at the party reaffirms the impossibility of escaping one's destiny: "La confusión que provocó ¿se engendró en el hecho de que se trataba de un intruso, que nadie sabía nada de él, que no había sido invitado y que primero con una mirada con que abarcó a todos y luego con jaque arrogancia sin pronunciar una palabra, hizo ademán ostensible de que no acudía allí para celebrar la fiesta sino más bien para aguarla?" (p. 110).

Another recurring symbol in *Un viaje* is the "espíritu de la porcelana" (pp. 30, 67, 123, 227, 231, etc.), which poignantly re-

[17]José Ortega, p. 254.

affirms the lack of anything permanent at La Gándara. As Demetria proclaims: "No, no quiero en mi casa porcelanas ni objetos de metal, nada que dure. Observa cómo aquí todo es inestable y putrescible, es como debe ser" (p. 91). Additional symbols which recur in *Un viaje* include the jackdaws, which are associated with the destiny of Arturo, the image of Demetria with her fingernails gripping the underside of the table (pp. 159, 167, 184, 185, 202), which is utilized to restrain the flow of time in chapter VI, and the transparent piece of paper with the single word AMAT (or TAMA) written on it, symbol of the dialectic between reason and instinct. Viewed as a whole, Benet's repeated use of symbols and leitmotivs significantly intensifies certain events and themes of the novel, while at the same time creates a rarefied atmosphere of ambiguity and uncertainty.

The enigmatic, impenetrable reality which characterizes both *Volverás a Región* and *Una meditación* reaches its most complex development in *Un viaje*, the last novel of Benet's trilogy on Región. The primary leitmotiv of *Un viaje* reflects the principal theme of all of Benet's previous novels: a destructive despair and ruin which permeates the physical background of Región and is reflected in the lives of the characters. In *Un viaje* this despair is intensified by the fatalistic destiny indicated in the title of the novel: a winter's journey in which the only reason for living lies in the path which leads toward death. For Arturo, death awaits in the forests of Mantua at the hands of Numa. For the other characters, death exists within life itself and takes root in the inability to escape their common destiny of solitude and despair.

In characteristic Benetian fashion, the stylistic features of *Un viaje* make the narrative nearly inaccessible to the reader. As Francisco Candel has observed concerning Benet's novels: "...una novela de Benet es muy buena, muy importante, pero imposible de penetrar más allá de la página quince."[18] However, Benet's style forms part of his whole elaborate method of presenting a complex reality which defies explicit presentation. As

[18]Cited in Darío Villanueva, "La novela de Juan Benet," *Camp de L'Arpa: Revista de Literatura*, N° 8 (noviembre de 1973), 9-16.

Darío Villanueva notes in his commentary on *Un viaje*: "La prosa de Benet es, en sus momentos de brillantez, un magnífico estudio de la inaprehensibilidad esencial de la realidad, que lejos de ser monolítica se presenta huidiza e inabarcable, incluso para un sujeto tan tópicamente lúcido como el narrador de una novela."[19] In *Un viaje* Benet reveals once again his predilection for eliminating plot and obliterating time. Similar to his previous novels, *Un viaje* reflects the mythical struggle of persons attempting to come to terms with a destiny which is filled with nothingness. In this sense, the lack of plot in the novel reinforces the characters' lack of progress toward discovering any kind of meaning in their lives, while the absence of a chronological time structure underscores the ambiguous existence of the characters and the monotonous routine of their lives. Thus in *Un viaje*, as in each of his previous novels, Benet succeeds in creating a novelistic reality based upon the rejection of traditional constructs in favor of a stylistic labyrinth in which characters and events are submerged in a dense fog of ambiguity and non-being.

[19]Darío Villanueva, p. 13.

LA OTRA CASA DE MAZON

Until now, the similarities between the novels of Faulkner and Benet are manifest primarily in terms of style: recurring motifs, oxymoronic constructions, ruptured syntax and peripatetic sentences appear repeatedly in the works of both authors. In fact, Benet has been familiar with the novels of Faulkner for nearly three decades. As he explains after being struck by the phrase, "My mother is a fish," when glancing through *As I Lay Dying*: "Acabo de descubrir a Faulkner (era la primavera de 1945), cuya lectura suspendí temporalmente el verano de 1967...."[1] In *La otra casa de Mazón* (1973), Benet's most recent novel, Faulknerian influence extends well beyond stylistic similarities. As in the American's *Requiem for a Nun* (1951), Benet's novel consists of interwoven sections of narrative and dramatic dialogue in the form of a play. However, whereas Faulkner's work consists of three acts, each of which is preceded by a lengthy prose introduction describing the historical background of the events, *La otra casa* consists of five sections each of prose and dialogue (including stage directions) which are intimately related by plot and thematic similarities. Indeed, a large portion of the drama serves either to clarify the ambiguity which characterizes the prose sections, or to enhance the themes of physical and psychological ruin which pervade the novel.

There is no plot in *La otra casa* in the traditional sense. Instead, the novel consists of a carefully selected series of events from the past and present which represent the decadence of the Mazón family. The house --"la otra casa de Mazón"[2]-- which is mentioned in the first sentence and recurs throughout the novel, forms the setting for both the drama and prose sections, and

[1]Juan Benet, "De Canudos a Macondo," *Revista de Occidente*, 2ª Serie, Vol. 24, Nº 70 (enero de 1969), 49-57.

[2]The title, *La otra casa de Mazón*, refers to the "other" Mazón household which exists in El Auge. In his previous novels, Benet has referred only to the Mazón family which lives in Región and fought in the Civil War.

138

therefore provides spatial unity and serves to intensify the themes of physical and psychological destructiveness. The action of the play takes place during the 1950's --"en el otoño de 1954 (y unos años antes y otros después)" [3]-- while the events of the narrative span a time period from mid-nineteenth century to near the end of the Civil War. Thus the narrative segments serve as an informational background to the play, allow Benet to introduce his thematic concerns by portraying the decadence of a once wealthy family and, primarily due to his style, enable him to create the ambience of despair and ruin which forms the essence of all of his novels.

Several major characteristics of Benet's previous novels form an integral part of *La otra casa*. For example, as in each of his previous novels, Benet treats time and memory in relation to human existence. Because of its ambiguous presentation, the chronological flow of time frequently becomes rarefied in Benet's novels. In *La otra casa*, the actual time span of many incidents, as well as the specific year or even decade in which they occur, remains uncertain. As discussed earlier, the play takes place in 1954 (or a few years before and afterwards), despite the fact that the stage directions do not specify changes in time. This temporal uncertainty is further enhanced by the reluctance of the narrator to designate a specific time for an occurrence. When relating the arrival of a letter at the Mazón house, for example, the narrator claims that "Unos días o una quincena más tarde llegó la otra comunicación..." (p. 151). A character's journey away from home lasts "dos o tres meses" (p. 75), while a baby is described as being born "uno o dos meses más tarde" (p. 65). Examined in isolation, the reticence of the narrator to specify the time seems relatively insignificant in the development of the novel. However, the recurring ambiguous temporal reference creates a pattern in both *La otra casa* and earlier novels which emphasizes Benet's desire to suggest realities rather than define them.

---

[3]Juan Benet, *La otra casa de Mazón* (Barcelona: Seix Barral, 1973), p. 29. Future references to *La otra casa...* will be from this edition and denoted in the text within parentheses.

The conflict between reason and instinct, which appears in varying degrees of intensity in each of Benet's novels, is also evident in *La otra casa*. As in his earlier works, Benet infuses his characters with a sexual desire which takes root in their natural (i.e., libidinal) energies, or "impulsos de la naturaleza" (p. 41). The medieval king, for example, is unable to escape his sexual desires even though he is dead: "¿Acaso no me despojé de los vínculos de la infancia y la influencia de los estímulos sexuales? Así, pues, al distraer la razón sólo he conseguido hacer independiente al apetito" (pp. 145-146). On the other hand, man still attempts to govern his society and existence by the inhibiting powers of his reason: "Y que el hombre persista en creer en la influencia del individuo. Que todavía actúe la fuerza que rige nuestros actos. Que todavía haya fe.... Que la raza humana siga creyendo en un orden dirigido por la razón..." (p. 155).

Benet has so far set the action of all of his novels in or around Región. In *La otra casa*, although the area bears the name El Auge, the geographic similarities between it and Región (which is also mentioned in the novel) clearly indicate that Benet wishes the reader to associate the two towns as part of the same spatial background. This fact is underscored by reference to several incidents, characters and geographic locations which have appeared before in Benet's novels. The Río Torce, of course, appears in each novel of the trilogy, and forms an integral part of *La otra casa* as both a witness and participant in the violent history of Región. To demonstrate further the historical continuity of his mythical region, Benet alludes to several events or persons from previous novels which play a part in the action of *La otra casa*. Dr. Sebastián, for example, appears in the novel in order to aid Eugenio Mazón, who is wounded near the end of the Civil War. In characteristic fashion, the Doctor is described as a pathetic, yet mysterious figure who suddenly appears at the Mazón house from out of nowhere: "En días sucesivos había de volver, en distintas ocasiones todas inopinadas, materialización instantánea de una nube que aprovechara el recelo ante la lluvia inminente para solidificarse en la figura enlutada con el paraguas y el cabás, que sin avanzar por el suelo encharcado, sin edad ni hora, volvía una y otra vez en miríadas de instantes repetidas por la curvatura del vacío de la reciente paz balanceándose en una acrónica

140

combinación de fatalidad y fortaleza y reconfortación" (pp. 201-202).

The enigmatic figure of Numa also surfaces in *La otra casa* as a sign of both the death which awaits the characters and as a symbol of the impenetrable forests of Mantua. Other references to previous novels include the group of Belgians who arrive in Región in hopes of plotting a map of Mantua (*Volverás a Región* and *Una meditación*), the fleeing figure of the *jugador* with several men in close pursuit (*Volverás a Región*), Eugenio Mazón fleeing into the mountains in 1938 to escape the Nationalist troops (*Volverás a Región* and *Una meditación*) and the allusions to events and battles of the Civil War (e.g., the battle of Loma, the fighting at the bridge) with the ultimate triumph of the Franco forces. Thus as one book leads to another, and Benet's mythical kingdom expands and grows more complex, the author alludes to incidents from other works and solidifies the overall pattern of his writing. As a result, Benet creates a strong bond between the geographical and psychological environment of his novels and the characters which move about within them. Similar to the manner in which Faulkner threads recurring incidents and characters through Yoknapatawpha County, Benet reintroduces people and events of Región and gives them life beyond the confines of a single work.

El Auge

The hermetic, frequently antagonistic atmosphere which characterizes the physical and psychological setting of Benet's novels permeates both the prose and dialogue sections of *La otra casa*. From the outset Benet portrays El Auge and the Mazón house in a complementary relationship of ruin and decay: "El lugar era apartado, inhóspito y malsano. Sólo una parte de la casa se mantenía todavía en pie, gracias en gran medida a su laxa, comprometida decadencia" (p. 11). El Auge is described in terms of solitude and loneliness, all that remain in the town after years of decay: "los muros de fachada carentes de interior, las contras abiertas y desplomadas que se abren a un montón de tejas y vigas calcinadas, un portal de mármol donde se preserva el único fresco estival de toda la comarca, la placa de un dentista, el letrero tricolor de un estanco... y los desflecados hilachos de unos paños que tras colgar años de un alambre han alcanzado la vida del espíritu" (pp. 12-13). The Mazón house itself also suggests a close affinity to Benet's previous works. Specifically, the decadent mansion which is portrayed in detail in the photographs of *Una tumba* is described verbally in *La otra casa*. The tangible wealth of the past is transformed into the emptiness of the present, which extends into the future and into eternity. Besieged by time and overrun by nature, the Mazón mansion represents all that is miserable and devoid of life in El Auge: "Y en poco tiempo una blanda y aislante capa de excremento y plumas y polvo y restos orgánicos vino a cubrir el más aparatoso exponente de una pasada riqueza con la propia sustancia del olvido, el sustento de la memoria una vez agotado el efímero apetito de independencia y su ficticio poder de regulación sobre una naturaleza animada de una voluntad sin designios, reducido de nuevo a la acumulación de pruebas materiales de leyes que, extraídas de la razón, contradictoriamente no la burlan porque tampoco la conciernen" (p. 190).

The threatening atmosphere of El Auge which the narrator portrays in the prose sections is amplified in the dramatic segments in a series of apostrophes by Yosen. Speaking to the earth as if it possessed life, Yosen condemns the area and the corrosive effects that it exercises on the inhabitants: "Miserable tierra, despojo de los mares que abandonaron tu incómodo lecho: estéril, adúltera, abominable asiento contra natura sin agua" (p. 140); "Tierra maldita y desierta..." (p. 134); "Agua maldita y amarga: siempre hay que buscarte en la oscuridad. Asoma de una vez y aprende a correr, agua pútrida, como tu hermano de más abajo" (p. 135); "Os conjuro a tí... tierra despreciable, tan sólo útil para la oración" (p. 142). The third person narrator likewise personifies the landscape and stresses the power of the Río Torce, which is "amplio y recio, tosco y rojo" (p. 14). In fact, the force of the river and its desire to recover lost territory aggravates the ruin of the Mazón mansion: "Cuando el viejo Mazón levantó su casa en el ribazo de enfrente, la ruina fue acelerada --a causa de la venganza del río dirigida hacia su propio santuario..." (p. 15).

In each of Benet's previous novels the destructive might of the landscape influences the psychological being of the characters. Although not portrayed directly in *La otra casa*, as in *Volverás a Región*, the relationship between the inhabitants and their environment is manifest in the lives of nearly all the members of the Mazón family. The mother of José, for example, restores the "silencio original" (p. 65) to an atmosphere which is dominated by "la casa degradada en el hastío" (p. 197). The ruinous effects of the house and all of El Auge are perhaps reflected most severely in Cristino, who is described at the beginning of the play as follows: "Su ropa está vieja y sucia y responde a una moda de veinte años atrás; los pantalones demasiado cortos dejan ver sus tobillos, no usa calcetines y sus zapatos de ante (sin pelo ni lustre con las puntas ennegrecidas) están surcados de profundas arrugas agujereadas que calan hasta los pies" (p. 33). The entire Mazón family plunges into ruin, with the exception of the elder Eugenio, who escapes the decadence of his family and El Auge by fleeing the town and establishing the other and more noble branch of Mazóns in nearby Región.

The overall effect of the atmosphere in *La otra casa* is perhaps best summarized by one of the characters in the play. The "Rey," who has been dead for nearly a thousand years but appears throughout the play in conversation with Cristino, describes succinctly the reality which surrounds the inhabitants of El Auge: "Todo lo que nos rodea [es un sueño]. Parece pendiente de un despertar. Es demasiado terrible para ser real. Debe haber un engaño por algún lado, alguien se preocupa de hacernos ver una faz más siniestra que la verdadera. Todo esto no es posible, Cris, ¿no crees tú?" (p. 106). However, the characters are not submerged in a deceptive dream, but rather in the harsh and hostile environment which has become the cornerstone of Benet's novels.

The Mazón Family

La otra casa presents a fragmented chronicle of the decline of the Mazón family. Similar to the novels of Faulkner in which the history of such famous literary families as the Compsons, Sutpens, Sartoris and Snopes is related in detail, the Mazón family tree becomes the subject for study and analysis by Benet. However, in contrast to Faulkner, who generally develops several family members to a high degree of complexity, Benet concentrates on only one character, Cristino Mazón, who appears as the central figure in the play and also merits detailed attention in the narrative. The other family members, however, appear and disappear throughout the novel and never gain full development as real human beings. Cristino, then, becomes the symbol of the entire Mazón family and personifies the theme of "ruin-in-life" which dominates the novel.

The genealogy of the Mazón family remains ambiguous in the novel, except that a form of degenerate in-breeding is suggested by the fact that several of the children have unknown fathers. Like Faulkner, Benet furnishes members of different generations with the same name: two sons called Carlos (first and fourth generation); three daughters named Clara (second, third and fourth generation) and two sons bear the name of Eugenio (second and fourth generation). In addition to these family members, the Mazón genealogical tree consists of Enrique ("el enfermo"), second generation and son of the "viejo Mazón;" Teresa, third generation; José, stepbrother of Eugenio, Enrique and Clara; Cristino; an unnamed son of the administrator's wife and Bruna, born in 1924, who becomes a prostitute. In total, thirteen children whose way of life gains tangible existence in Cristino, the only known Mazón to remain alive in the 1950's.[4]

As discussed earlier, Cristino Mazón appears in the play in a state of almost complete poverty; he is dressed in tattered clothes and wears worn-out shoes. Nonetheless, he maintains about him an air of aristocratic supremacy: "Aunque descuidado, conserva un cierto aire distinguido; un hombre vencido pero que no se abandona y alimenta, empero, ese aire de indefinible e invicto orgullo --patente cuando se contempla las uñas a distancia-- de quien no ha trabajado nunca" (p. 33). His attitude of superiority becomes patently obvious in his treatment of Eugenia,

---

[4]See pages 65-67 for a detailed description of four generations of the Mazón family.

his former mistress and servant who is now too old to arouse the
same sexual excitement as in the past. Cristino's frequent allusions to the difference in social class between him and Eugenia
form a recurring motif in the novel and enhance his ironic character portrayal. The following passages typify Cristino's patroniz-
ing attitude:

> Entre tú y yo hay una insalvable diferencia de cla-
> se social. Que tengamos que sufrir la misma suerte es
> una inconveniencia que algunas tardes me llena de re-
> pugnancia y me arrastra al borde de la desesperación.
> (p. 49)

> No pretendas averiguar mis pensamientos. No
> quiero entrar en detalles, soy de clase superior. Supe-
> rior en todo, ¿me escuchas Eugenia? (p. 36)

> La fatalidad no es cosa para la gente humilde. Para
> gente de baja extracción, como tú. ¿Te das cuenta,
> Eugenia, de que te estoy hablando? (p. 37)

> Las clases altas hemos de sufrir con dignidad vues-
> tro rencor. No cabe hablar de despecho con vosotros.
> Todas nuestras concesiones las interpretáis como de-
> bilidad; y cobardía lo que es generosidad. ¿A mí qué
> me importa lo que tú creas? (p. 38)

> El miedo, Eugenia, es privilegio de unos pocos; de
> los que somos de cuna. Cada día estoy más convenci-
> do de que eso es todo, la cuna, la alcurnia. Vosotros
> no tenéis nada, ni vergüenza; la gente ordinaria, la
> masa, ni siquiera tiene miedo. (p. 57)

> Todos los de clase humilde sois iguales. Gente sin
> alegría, sin imaginación.... (p. 59)

Cristino's denigration of Eugenia is extremely ironic, of
course, because the two characters live in the same state of decadence and share the same ruined mansion at El Auge. Indeed,
Cristino's insistence that Eugenia is inferior because she belongs
to a lower social class represents more of an effort to convince
himself of something that he urgently needs to believe. The irony
is further enhanced by Cristino's assertion that the power of his
lineage still exists in El Auge, and instills fear into the inhabitants: "Mi raza está hecha para dominar, Eugenia, para sojuz-
gar. Hemos dominado el siglo y, en el fondo --fíjate qué noche

tan negra se avecina--, nos siguen temiendo" (p. 41). However, the Mazóns neither maintain dominance in the area --they are all dead except Cristino-- nor do any residents remain in El Auge to fear the once powerful family.

Cristino's personality is developed in both the narrative and dramatic sections of the novel, with the former supplying information from the past which helps to explain his dialogue in the present. The vision of the world which Cristino imparts throughout the play can perhaps best be described as a negation of normally accepted and estimable personality traits. When Eugenia laments that Yosen possesses no hope for the future, Cristino claims, "Tanto mejor. Tampoco [las esperanzas] me quedan a mí y mira cómo me conservo" (p. 42). Concerning his fellow human beings Cristino asserts that, "Con todo, esa mezcla de bondad y resolución en la mirada... no conozco nada peor. A mí dadme gente a cuyo rostro asome la maldad" (p. 181). And he later adds: "¿El linaje humano? La envidia, Eugenia, la envidia" (p. 229). Cristino also insists that he is a "moral" person, yet his words belie the morality which he professes: "Porque cuando se tiene una moral tan rígida como la mía, yo creo que no se puede mover un dedo. No se puede hacer nada, nada: todo está mal" (p. 50); "Y te digo que da igual porque una moral rígida como la mía no permite esas ridículas distinciones entre lo bueno y lo malo. Quede eso para las personas ambiciosas. Una moral rígida y una confianza absoluta en que, en esencia, no ocurrirá nunca nada" (pp. 51-52). Thus Cristino portrays by his own words the overwhelming sense of degradation in which he lives, and creates powerful dramatic irony due to his distorted self-concept.

In contrast to Faulkner's desire "to create flesh-and-blood people that will stand up and cast a shadow,"[5] Benet frequently creates characters which seem to exist in a state of non-being. In *La otra casa*, Benet's predilection for ethereal characters is readily apparent at the beginning of the play. According to the author, the characters include Cristino Mazón, Eugenia Fernández, Alejandro Lassa, Yosen, a King, "Y otras figuras, semidesnudas e ininteligibles, que pertenecieron o pertenecían a la familia y tra-

[5]William Faulkner, cited in Olga W. Vickery, *The Novels of William Faulkner* (Baton Rouge: Louisiana State University Press, 1964), p. 295.

146

ídas a la memoria porque también, irremediablemente, seguían habitando o merodeando la casa" (p. 29).

Within the body of the play several of these "figuras borrosas" are deceased members of the Mazón family, who return to the house because of their hatred of Cristino. Near the end of the work we discover that Cristino was responsible either directly or indirectly for the deaths of several of his brothers and relatives. Many of these incidents are portrayed in the prose sections, but in typical Benetian fashion, the persons involved and the eventual outcome remain shrouded in mystery and uncertainty. The best developed and most complex of these incidents concerns Cristino and his older brother, Eugenio, during two different moments of the characters' lives. As a child, the younger Cristino never became fully integrated with the other children in their daily playing of games and other activities. Instead, he remained close to his mother and frequently informed her when the other children were misbehaving. One day when playing hide-and-seek, Cristino hides in the attic of the garage, where Eugenio is unable to find him. Encouraged by his success at eluding his brother, Cristino next moves into the grain storage attic where the children normally enter only when accompanied by an adult. Cristino is successful in his desire not to be found, but as the day wears on he becomes trapped in the darkened room and surrounded by a pack of rats. Frightened to such a degree that he loses his senses, Cristino is saved by the appearance of the "hombre con un sombrero de fieltro,"[6] who enters the room carrying a lantern and frightens the rats away. However, Cristino is scarred for life by the violent reaction of one of the creatures:

> Todos los animales echaron a correr, a excepción de uno que --subido al pubis del niño--, demasiado interesado en su presa para soltarla por tan somera admonición, hizo ademán de defenderla --abandonada ya por todos su congéneres-- agitando su hocico y sus

[6]The "hombre con el sombrero de fieltro negro" appears twice in the novel: once to frighten away the rats, and another time at the Mazón house when the children are playing outside. In the latter incident, the man inexplicably appears and disappears out of nowhere. Immediately afterward, the son of the administrator loses his fear of fire and is burned to death.

bigotes, lanzando un chillido y mostrando los dientes, de los que se desprendió una pequeña pieza de te-
la impregnada de sangre y con briznas de paja y fi-
bras de carne adheridas a ella, para, a seguido, emi-
tir un ronquido en son de amenaza. (pp. 195-196)

The second incident involving the rats centers upon Eugenio
during the Civil War. Wounded during a battle with the Nationalist troops, Eugenio seeks refuge in his former household, where
Cristino and Eugenia are the only inhabitants. Fearing that Eugenio will be discovered by the Nationalists, Cristino hides his
older brother in the grain attic, the same place where Cristino
was attacked as a youth. During the night Eugenio is killed by
the rats in a scene reminiscent of Cristino's experience:

La rendija de la luz de la puerta abierta sobre el
montón de sacos hizo correr varios cuerpos invisibles
en pos de las fugitivas tinieblas, pero una de ellas que
aún tratara de defender su botín se encaró con el intruso mostrando sus colmillos y agitando sus bigotes
al tiempo que lanzaba el chillido: a una patada en el
suelo se encaramó hasta su cabeza, reclinada sobre la
pila de sacos, como para cubrir y disimular aquella
mitad del cráneo que había sido despojada de todo pelo y que, desmoronada, semejaba el arrumbado mani-
quí de un peluquero, que mostrara por el contraste
con la mitad calva el efecto rejuvenecedor del postizo.
(p. 204)

The two scenes described above --first with Cristino and later
with Eugenio-- form an integral part of *La otra casa* from both a
thematic and technical point of view. From the standpoint of
technique, the two incidents enhance the ambiguous nature of
the narrative because the characters involved are never alluded
to by name. In the first scene, the narrator refers to a "niño" or
"hermano," while in the second he alludes to "un herido." Only
later in the dramatic segments do we discover the protagonists of
each incident, and then only by associating the two brothers
with the image of the rat. Furthermore, Benet's use of the rat in
La otra casa is similar to that in *Una meditación*, in which the
ambiguity of certain scenes is clarified later in the novel by link-
ing the animal to Jorge Ruan and Camila. In *La otra casa* the rat

is mentioned early in the novel by Clara when speaking to Cristino: "...y Eugenio, que te trae una rata" (p. 96). However, the identity of the two characters is made clear only when Clara refers to Eugenio's "muerte en el sobrado" (p. 226) near the end of the novel. In *La otra casa*, therefore, as occurs frequently in Benet's works, incidents are clarified not by straightforward exposition, but rather by the active participation of the reader in piecing together the puzzle-like fragments which compose the novel.

From a thematic perspective the two scenes poignantly demonstrate the isolation of Cristino from his brothers and sisters and his subsequent desire for revenge. Cristino knows that Eugenio will die in the grain attic, but not before experiencing the same helpless fear which Cristino suffered in the room several years before (when hiding from Eugenio). Cristino's thirst for vengeance, which stems from his ostracism by his brothers and sisters, can most accurately be described in terms of the Cain complex. This theme, which is developed most intensely in Spain by Unamuno, appears in *La otra casa* as a kind of primitive impulse in Cristino's nature which forces him to vie for recognition from others. When this recognition is not forthcoming, and when he is rejected instead, Cristino strikes back with such viciousness that he creates a fratricidal war in which he alone is the victor. Not only does he cause the death of Eugenio, but he is also connected in some manner to the death or ruin of Carlos, José, Clara, Bruna and Serafín. Thus Cristino not only symbolizes the ruin of a family, but also constitutes one of the principal forces behind its destruction.

One additional character which merits attention in *La otra casa* is the medieval king, who is mentioned only briefly in the first narrative segment (p. 13), but plays a major role in the dramatic dialogue. Whereas Cristino Mazón personifies the negative traits of modern man and symbolizes the decadence of a family, the king incarnates the objectionable features of the past and shares the ruin of the Mazón family in the present. Like Cristino, the king possesses a pessimistic vision of the world: "El mal está en base de todo, no se puede desarraigar" (p. 162). The king also derides the innate being of mankind by claiming that "la pobreza, la resignación, constituyen nuestra natural forma de ser" (p. 211). In part, the king's presence in the novel serves as a demythification of history. Instead of the noble figure of the medieval ruler who champions the path of righteousness, Benet's king appears as a hypocritical figure who would not exchange the present day comforts for the lofty values of the past. Thus while the king is "un símbolo de la historia" (p. 105), everything that he eulogizes --sexual exploitation, the torture of heretics, the massacre of people in small towns-- vitiates his position of royalty and destroys the myths of yesteryear. On the other hand, the objects which he scorns --"el afán de justicia" (p. 100); "la juventud [que] quiere una vida más digna, más limpia y ordenada" (p. 159)-- are representative of contemporary society and the values of democracy. Thus Benet's social criticism, which usually appears indirectly and subtly, becomes clearly manifest in the figure of the repugnant medieval king.

The characters of *La otra casa*, especially as they appear in the dialogue, create a surrounding reality of relative absurdity. Much of the dialogue involves the repetition of words and ideas (e.g., the class difference between Cristino and Eugenia, the constant reference to noises outside the house, the extinguished sexual prowess of Eugenia), and at times Benet seems to utilize language in the characteristic absurdist fashion of "non-communication" between people. Perhaps the king describes the dialogue most accurately when he asserts that "Nuestra conversación no tiene el menor interés" (p. 186). In addition, Benet enhances the absurd nature of the characters by allowing the reader to catch glimpses of the ghost-like members of the Mazón family, who appear out of nowhere in their former house at El Auge. With obvious ironic humor, Cristino comments on the general atmosphere of the house by insisting that: "Aquí sólo hemos percibido la calma de todos los días. Todo parece en orden, no veo qué razón hay para inquietarse" (p. 85).[7] On the other hand, the narrator's portrayal of the Mazón family aids in explaining the tragic circumstances in which they encounter themselves. In all of Benet's novels the characters are trapped in a suffocating atmo-

---

[7]I do not mean to imply here, however, that Cristino is aware of the irony of his statement. In fact, he is totally oblivious to the ironic nature of much of what he says.

150

sphere of ruin and despair and, although not creatures "de carne y hueso," experience distressingly real problems and suffer real anguish.

Style and Technique

The prose segments of *La otra casa* are told from the point of view of a third person narrator. Contrary to Thomas Franz's assertion that these sections are "narrated in a traditional omniscient manner,"[8] the narrator of *La otra casa* appears reticent to utilize omniscience to relate the action. In fact, this unwillingness appears to some degree in all of Benet's novels. As Darío Villanueva notes, "[Benet] no pretende, salvo en esporádicas descripciones francamente objetivistas, un ocultamiento del autor, pero sí la destrucción de su omnisciencia."[9] In *Volverás a Región* Benet treats the problem with ironic humor: the narrator is unable to name Rumbal (Robal, Rubal, Rembal, etc.) accurately. In *Una meditación* first person omniscience is mitigated by the narrator's repeated assertion that he cannot be certain of what he is narrating, while in *Un viaje de invierno* the narrator frequently qualifies what he says with such remarks as "tal vez," "parece que," etc. In *La otra casa* this reluctance appears throughout the novel as the narrator repeatedly inserts such comments as "es posible," "al parecer," "tal vez," "acaso," etc., all of which undermine traditional omniscience and reveal the narrator's uncertain knowledge. Also, of course, any eagerness to specify or label without qualification would be antithetical to Benet's overall stylistic and technical purpose of withholding information and suggesting, rather than defining, the elements which form his novelistic reality.

The differences in style between the prose and dialogue segments of *La otra casa* could not be more pronounced. The play,

[8]Thomas Franz, review of *La otra casa de Mazón* by Juan Benet, *Journal of Spanish Studies: Twentieth Century*, Vol. 2, No. 2 (Fall, 1973), 197-198.

[9]Darío Villanueva, "La novela de Juan Benet," *Camp de L'Arpa: Revista de Literatura*, N° 8 (noviembre de 1973), 9-16.

which consists of five sections of dialogue, is characterized by a straightforward and succinct manner of speech which is highly realistic in terms of syntax and word usage. In contrast, the dense, circumlocutory style of writing which marks each of Benet's previous novels appears in the narrative segments of *La otra casa* with characteristic intensity and complexity.

One of the principal achievements of Benet's style lies in the author's ability to draw the reader into the flow and rhythm of his words as they interanimate. In *La otra casa*, Benet frequently amasses words in order to describe as accurately as possible the complex reality which he portrays at any particular moment. Most commonly, he compounds words into groups of three, and thereby gives depth and multiformity to his descriptions. In order not to belabor this point, I will concentrate on one section of prose which extends from pages 189-204. Within this fifteen-page segment nouns, adjectives and verbs appear in series of three on twelve separate occasions. Benet uses this technique for three fundamental purposes: 1) it gives his prose a rhythmic fluidity; 2) it enables him to suggest fine nuances of meaning; 3) it allows him to emphasize a singular description or event. Two examples will serve to distinguish between the latter two categories. The pigeons which inhabit the abandoned garage of the Mazón house view an old carriage with "ebúrneo, somnoliento y protocolario despego" (p. 189). When describing the feeling of emptiness in one of his characters, the narrator asserts that the person is submerged in an "abyecto y creciente y sin límites vacío" (p. 195). In the first example, each of the three adjectives provides a varied description of the indifference with which the birds regard the carriage. The ivory-colored, somnolent and judiciary modifiers suggest distinctive shades of meaning which considerably enhance the total effect of the image. In the second example, however, Benet utilizes the adjectives for intensification. The first modifier, "abyecto," suggests the psychological state of mind, while the final two expand the immeasurability of the emptiness. Thus instead of portraying delicate distinctions in meaning, as with the first example, Benet uses the latter series of adjectives to stress and reinforce the psychological state which he is trying to create.

The use of nouns in groups of three is also a common stylistic trait of the novel. In the narrative segment of our immediate attention, nouns are grouped together principally in order to underscore and amplify, as opposed to distinguishing subtleties of meaning. For example, the aftermath of the Civil War is characterized by "heridas y venganzas y resquemores" (p. 191); the decadence of the storeroom is evident by the clearly visible "excrementos y plumas y restos de pájaros" (p. 193); the silence of the mansion is magnified by "una masa de broza y una caballería muerta y un camión inutilizado" (p. 197) while the decaying body of Eugenio emits "un intenso tufo a fiebre, sed y sudor" (p. 199). By continually amassing the nouns in certain descriptive situations, Benet achieves a completeness of expression which enhances the overall force of his narrative style.

The influence of Faulkner in the style of *La otra casa* can also be seen in the use of oxymoronic constructions and ethereal descriptions. As in his previous novel, *Un viaje de invierno*, Benet portrays characters in a state of non-being. For example, Clara's first affair with an unknown admirer is described as follows: "...en una noche de verano en la que un murmullo tras una cortina, una mano que a través de la rendija de la puerta le apretó la muñeca y una sombra no discernible entre los olmos, le invitaron a gozar de la calma de la hora y del frescor del río, en la otra margen, en las ruinas del monasterio" (p. 76). Later Clara appears (or disappears) when she disrobes in front of her lover: "no bien fue desnudada... pareció esfumarse sin dejar otra seña --ni el calor del cuerpo, ni el rumor de una palabra, ni el aliento ni la ausencia del tacto, ni la sensación de su peso, ni la visión en sombras de sus facciones..." (pp. 128-129). Similar devices which enhance the portrayal of an ethereal reality include the pseudo-oxymoronic description "el zumbido sin ruido ni origen" (p. 127) associated with the silence of the house, or the portrayal of the stables, which "vertían su oquedad a través de las juntas y grietas de las tablas, y aquellas puertas y mallas cerradas --tan débiles y firmes al mismo tiempo--..." (p. 193). This intangible, rarefied ambience stands in direct contrast to the palpable physical decadence of the Mazón family and property. Therefore, these two antithetical realities, by virtue of their contradictory qualities, create a tenebrous dissonance which characterizes both the form and content of the novel.

Although the commingling of narrative and dramatic dialogue in a single novel represents a significant departure from Benet's previous works, the two techniques and styles of writing by themselves are by no means new for Benet. He had previously published a collection of plays, *Teatro* (1971),[10] while the narrative style of *La otra casa* clearly takes root in his prior novels. However, the juxtaposition of the two techniques provides Benet with broad flexibility in the development of his work. For example, the two intertwining parts portray different time periods in the tale of the Mazón family. Furthermore, by permitting several of the characters to speak for themselves, Benet amplifies the perspective of his third person narrator with diverse points of view. Yet Darío Villanueva has perhaps described most precisely the effect of combining the narrative and dialogue when he suggests that "el drama es algo así como un descanso para el lector."[11] For the reader familiar with Benet's novels, the relative simplicity of the dialogue offers a welcome relief from the dense prose of the narrative.

On occasion in *La otra casa*, as in his earlier novels, Benet creates sharp, piercing images with a minimum of words. The setting sun, for example, "[extraía] del ladrillo el color de su interior" (p. 17), and the scratches on the chest of Carlos are depicted concisely by the "tímidas y espaciadas gotas de sangre que con desgana acudieron a presenciar el espectáculo" (p. 150). In general, however, the words flow in torrents in *La otra casa*, and Benet exploits fully their cumulative power and energy. Repeatedly in the novel Benet displays a predilection for marathon sentences and complicated syntax and, as discussed above, the use of words in a series contributes significantly to the intensity of meaning and rhythmic effluence which typify his use of language.[12]

---

[10]Juan Benet, *Teatro* (Madrid: Siglo Veintiuno de España Editores, 1971). The three plays in the collection are entitled, *Anastas o el origen de la Constitución, Agonía Confutans* and *Un caso de conciencia.*

[11]Darío Villanueva, pp. 10-11.

[12]Benet's predilection for grouping words into three's or four's is not peculiar to

Benet portrays the characters of *La otra casa* in his normal ambiguous fashion. Nearly all the members of the Mazón family appear as phantasmagorical beings, while only Cristino and the medieval king are developed in detail. Through these two characters Benet enhances his central theme of ruin by associating the dead king --killed by the Moors during the Reconquest-- with the decay of the Mazón family during the twentieth century. The two characters represent essentially the same idea --decadence-- and Benet implies that the history of Spain can be viewed as a process of slow, but continual ruination. On the other hand, Benet seems to question the whole process of life and history, symbolized by the game of dominoes which the characters play throughout the drama. Is there a foreordained pattern which controls our life? In his previous novels Benet suggests that there is, and creates for his characters (Dr. Sebastián, Arturo, Demetria, the "niño," etc.) a predetermined destiny which is futile to resist. In *La otra casa*, however, the author appears to vacillate. Although the characters are waiting for something --we don't know what-- which seems inevitable, the game they are playing implies that chance will affect the eventual outcome of their lives. As Cristino notes, "Quizá el remedio esté en el juego" (p. 47). Thus in contrast to his previous novels, Benet mitigates the deterministic influence and increases the role of fortune in the life and destiny of his characters.[13]

La otra casa de Mazón. Ricardo Gullón has noted this characteristic in *Volverás a Región*, and a detailed study of Benet's other novels reveals a similar tendency.

[13]Despite the importance given to "azar" in the novel, Benet engulfs the characters in their *race* and *milieu*, and the members of the Mazón family seem to be destined to a tragic life and death.

CONCLUSION

Although it would be precipitate to propose any definitive con-
clusions concerning Benet's novels as a completed corpus of material, certain observations can be made which will elucidate
what he has achieved in his writing to the present time. We must
therefore attempt to identify what Henry James called "The Figure in the Carpet," "the thing that most makes [the writer] ap-
ply himself, the thing without the effort to achieve which he
wouldn't write at all, the very passion of his passion, the part of
the business in which, for him, the flame of art burns most intensely." Certainly, neither Benet's uniqueness nor the flame of
his art is to be found within the tradition of post-war realism. On
the contrary, Benet has repeatedly criticized the post-war realists
for their lack of stylistic and esthetic concerns. Benet's own theories, in contrast, reveal a preoccupation with style and art for
art's sake, and his novels constitute an unequivocal reification of
his protests against the novel of the last three decades. Like the
French new novelists, Benet writes complex novels which are the
antithesis of the popular "novels of consumption." Indeed, he
intentionally writes for a minority of people: "No me importa la
amenidad. Hay que escribir para pocos. Quizá para uno. En
cuanto el escritor se guía por el público está perdido."[1] Since Benet does not write for the masses, he is clearly not *engagé* in a
Sartrian sense. Rather, he is *comprometido* in the manner of the
nouveau roman: "Yo estoy comprometido conmigo mismo. Comprometido es una obligación moral derivada de otro u otros. No
me gusta la palabra comprometido. Prefiero compulsado. Compulsado es la obligación de todo tipo nacido de uno."[2]

The fundamental question persists, however, as to what gen-
uinely distinguishes Benet as a writer for the elite; a writer
whose novels are difficult to read, let alone understand; a writer

[1]Miguel Fernández Braso, "Juan Benet: un talento excitado," in *De escritor a
escritor* (Barcelona: Editorial Taber, 1970), p. 200.

[2]Miguel Fernández Braso, p. 203.

who has claimed that "la gloria de un escritor descansa en la facultad de seguir siendo un motivo de gozo para la clase culta."[3] In short, what is the figure which Benet is weaving in his still incomplete carpet? In the first place, the extreme difficulty of Benet's works stems from what some critics have designated "la escritura secreta" or "la escritura singularizante": the enigmatic and inexplicable nature of nearly all of his novels. As we have seen throughout our study, Benet utilizes a Faulknerian-like style replete with marathon sentences, labyrinthine syntax, esoteric vocabulary and an intricate system of images, the aim of which is two-fold: 1) to distinguish certain nuances of meaning or denote the complexity of actions and events; 2) to withhold meaning deliberately in order to keep the form and content of the novel fluid and unfinished. Like Faulkner, Benet offers obstacles, obtrusions and confusing digressions in his novels which discourage the passive reader but challenge the active one. However, one pronounced difference between the novels of Benet and Faulkner reveals an underlying contrast in their approach to writing. Whereas a novel of Faulkner may be extremely difficult to untangle, the intelligent reader will be able to overcome the obstacles in his path and understand the work because Faulkner furnishes (albeit indirectly) all the necessary information. Benet, on the other hand, not only imposes barriers, but by means of delaying or partially disclosing certain incidents and ideas, he in effect forecloses the possibility of total understanding of his work. What motivates Arturo to ascend the Río Torce in *Un viaje de invierno*? Why is the young boy doomed to suffer the revenge of the Brigadier in *Una tumba*? What happens between Leo and Carlos Bonaval during their trip into the mountains in *Una meditación*? Does the omnipresent figure of Numa really exist and, if so, why and how does he stalk the forests of Mantua? These and a score of other questions remain unanswered in Benet's novels, primarily, I believe, because they represent the author's view that many facets of our existence defy rational cognition. Through his use of magical realism, the mysterious

---

[3]Cited in Sergio Gómez Parra, "Juan Benet: la ruptura de un horizonte novelístico," *Reseña*, 9 (1972), 3-12.

power of destiny, *azar* and insoluble psychic enigmas, Benet creates an abstruse reality in his novels which frequently remains impenetrable.

Benet's preoccupation with time also forms part of the figure in the carpet. His temporal conception in part determines the structure of his novels, while at the same time it constitutes one of his recurring thematic concerns. In all of his novels Benet sets at least part of the action specifically during the Spanish Civil War, and thus gives an external point of reference to the work. However, the psychological portrayal of time destroys all semblance of the chronological flow of events. Objectively, Benet believes time exists and weaves its pattern regardless of the presence or absence of any one individual. This idea is readily apparent in the symbol of the clock in *Una meditación*, the decayed mansion in *Una tumba* or the cycles of time indicated by the change of season in *Un viaje de invierno*. Most commonly, however, Benet focuses on subjective time in which the ticking of a clock has no meaning, and months and years lose their independent value and fuse with the psychological flow of the human mind.

As Olga Vickery has accurately stated, "Though man's measurement of time is logical, his comprehension of it depends not only on reason but on memory and hope. The former defines his past while the latter anticipates his future."[4] Although Benet's characters frequently are able to remember, hope rarely surfaces. When it does exist, as in the case of Gamallo's daughter, it is quickly extinguished. In essence, the characters of Benet's novels have no hope for the future because their entire life consists of "un podría-haber-sido." This theme, which appears repeatedly in post-war Spanish literature, is intensified in Benet to such a degree that the future becomes decapitated by an overwhelming sense of fatalism which emanates from the past. Benet's characters do not grow as time passes, but rather remain stagnant. Through the process of antipathetic symbiosis they become absorbed by the decadence in which they are always submerged. The material ruin of the atmosphere thus parallels the intellectu-

---

[4]Olga Vickery, *The Novels of William Faulkner* (Baton Rouge: Louisiana State University Press, 1964), p. 257.

al degeneration of the inhabitants.

The ruin which forms a leitmotiv in all of Benet's novels for the individual characters must also be viewed on a national level. From the standpoint of the entire country, the mythical Región represents for Spain what Faulkner's Yoknapatawpha County symbolizes for Southern United States: a microcosm of the social, political and existential problems which confront man in his contemporary state of being. In the novels of Benet, the Civil War provides a backdrop against which a large portion of the action is staged, and the author casts a critical eye on both sides of the political spectrum. If the Republican period of the 1930's was characterized by a group of inept leaders who lacked the skill and foresight to rule the country, the Nationalist victors have done nothing to improve the situation. Benet portrays the nation after the war as a diseased body with the prognosis of a slow and painful death. As Dr. Sebastián insists in *Volverás a Región*, the Civil War was fought in order to lose it, to destroy Spain in order to rebuild it. However, instead of reconstructing the country both physically and spiritually, Franco has succeeded only in creating a state of mental paralysis in which the inability to think or to act independently is summed up in the oft-heard phrase, "Estamos tranquilos." For Benet the Spaniards are tranquil because of the *abulia* which permeates their minds and forces them to accept their destiny.

The ruin and decadence which is depicted sporadically in relation to the Civil War grows intense when the author portrays Región. Benet first introduces the reader to Región (and to the recurring figure of Dr. Sebastián) in his short story, "Baalbec, una mancha" (*Nunca llegarás a nada*, 1961), but does not describe it in detail until *Volverás a Región*. Beginning with a "realistic," objective description of the geographic details of the area, Benet then proceeds to anthropomorphize Región by infusing it with an air of hostility and a mysterious power of destruction. This suffocating spatial background appears with equal magnitude and force (although with less description) in each of Benet's novels and forms the central motif in the carpet which Benet weaves of Región and its inhabitants.

Another recurring preoccupation of Benet is manifest in the conflict between reason and instinct. Like Freud, Benet sees man trapped by his need to fulfill the instinctual desires of his libidinal energies in a society which prohibits such fulfillment. Although he vacillates concerning the ultimate resolution of the problem, Benet attacks the repressive nature of civilized society. This is especially evident on a general level in *Volverás a Región*, in which he vitiates the sacrosanct idea of the family as "la trampa de la razón" (p. 137). On an individual level, Benet treats the problem most explicitly in *Una meditación*, where the characters attempt to fulfill their erotic desires and achieve happiness through genital intercourse. They fail, of course, because they lack the essential ingredients of love and affection necessary to establish lasting erotic relationships. Yet as we have pointed out previously, there is nothing erotic about Benet's novels despite the frequency with which he discusses the subject of sex. His treatment of sex usually reads as if it was based on the abstractions and theories of a psychoanalytic textbook rather than on real characters of flesh and blood. Thus his presentation of instinct (primarily in the form of eros and sex), like nearly everything else in his novels, stems from his singular, rarefied view of reality and the persons who move about within it.

As we have shown in our analysis of the individual novels, Benet's style parallels that of William Faulkner in several significant ways. Indeed, Benet can perhaps be described most accurately (like Faulkner) as a verbal voluptuary: his words flood the page in torrents and interanimate with energetic zeal. At times, the sheer quantity of words in a sentence challenges the reader to follow the central idea, which frequently becomes submerged among the numerous subordinate clauses, parentheses and subparentheses. However, as Benet has matured as a writer and gained greater control over language, he has mitigated the intricate and frequently burdensome nature of his prose. While maintaining the essential elusiveness of his manner of writing, he has achieved a steady "aligeración" of his style which is first evident in *Un viaje de invierno* and further refined in *La otra casa de Mazón*. In each of these novels Benet reduces the length of his sentences and constricts the peripatetic nature of his style to provide an equally complex, yet linguistically more accessible work of fiction.

Benet and the Contemporary Spanish Novel

Since style forms such an integral part of his theory of literature (see chapter II), Benet objects to novels (and novelists) which demonstrate little concern for stylistic development. For this reason Benet rejects nearly all of the Realistic and Naturalistic novels of the nineteenth century as being deficient in literary value. As he writes concerning the latter school of authors: "Pero ni Zola ni Galdós lograron encontrar la libertad que concede el lenguaje artístico: el *dictat* sociológico redactaba todos sus párrafos de tal suerte que sólo hicieron una novela asertórica, exactamente esa clase horrible de novela que la sociedad --no demasiado enterada de la necesidad de una obra así-- esperaba que hiciese."[5] Benet denounces the common nineteenth-century practice according to which an author chooses a subject for his novel, and subsequently studies the subject by firsthand observation and scientific analysis over a long period of time. Such writing is not literature, insists Benet, but rather sociology.

It comes as no surprise, therefore, that Benet also regards the post-war Spanish novel of objective realism with such disfavor. He claims that the Spanish novel in general since the time of Galdós lacks literary excellence because it exhibits concern neither with style nor with the mysterious elements which lie beneath the surface of reality. In fact, Benet insists that the twentieth-century neorealistic novel in Spain is merely a form of *costumbrismo*:

> ...la novela de hoy, la de ayer y la de anteayer, es una novela que le falta imaginación y que, aceptando en cada momento el dictado moral, el escritor español no ha salido de cierto costumbrismo muy romo. Y eso, sea en la novela de estampas, en la novela de costumbres, en la novela de denuncia social, ha estado siempre limitado a un tipo de narración demasiado sujeto a la vida cotidiana. En este país no ha habido, yo creo que desde el siglo XIX, novela de aventura, novela de misterio, novela de mar --excepto Baroja--,

[5]Juan Benet, "Reflexiones sobre Galdós," *Cuadernos para el Diálogo*, Número Extraordinario XXIII (diciembre de 1970), p. 13.

ni novela de imaginación: y, si me apuras, ni novela de pasión. No ha habido más que estampas de la vida familiar, de la vida provinciana, de la vida en el campo y de la vida en la oficina.... A mí no me interesa. Cambio todo Galdós por una novela de Stevenson.[6]

While rejecting the post-war realistic novel, Benet has emerged during the last five years as an imposing symbol of the radical change in attitude in Spain toward prose fiction. Whereas the writer of post-war realism attempted to reflect or reproduce the reality in which he lived, Benet is concerned primarily with inventing his own reality. He creates the enigmatic spatial background of his novels by puncturing the surface of existence and revealing the complex, frequently abstruse reality hidden beneath the external elements portrayed by the neorealists. Furthermore, whereas the Generation of 1950 generally displayed a single vision and purpose in their novels as a result of their *engagé* attitude, Benet opts for a multifarious view which stems from his desire for artistic freedom. However, Benet's *desengagé* attitude is not as antithetical to the novelistic tradition which precedes him as some critics (as well as Benet himself) have suggested. On the contrary, while rejecting the narrow vision and traditional style of writing of the Generation of 1950, Benet attacks (although in a different fashion) many of the same problems. He threads a commentary on the disastrous effects of the Civil War throughout all of his novels, and decries repeatedly the lack of *voluntad* which has vanquished his country. Benet is not, therefore, a *desengagé* writer, nor is he *engagé* in the totally committed, Sartrian sense. Instead, the social criticism in his novels surfaces indirectly as part of his whole elaborate creation of "una región laberíntica que bien pudiera llamarse España."

While the Generation of 1950 was influenced to a large extent by the Italian neorealists, the American Lost Generation and the centuries-old Spanish tradition of realism, Benet has been most affected in his writing by Faulkner, Melville, Conrad, Stevenson

---

[6]Juan Benet, Interview with Antonio Núñez, "Encuentro con Juan Benet," *Insula*, Vol. 24, N° 269 (abril de 1969), 4.

162

and a number of Latin American writers. In fact, he applauds the new novelists of Latin America for their part in revolutionizing the novel of the Spanish language: "La literatura iberoamericana nunca me había atraído demasiado y me había convencido muy poco por un no sé qué de rudimentaria.... Pero de repente todo ha cambiado... y me ha venido a descubrir que en menos de diez años han surgido de la América española los ejemplares más notables de la narrativa castellana.... Ahí están: Rulfo en México, Carpentier en Cuba, Vargas en Perú y, por último, este asombroso García Márquez. Nada en castellano se ha escrito en 30 años comparable a *El reino de este mundo*, *Pedro Páramo*, *La casa verde*, *Cien años de soledad* o *El coronel no tiene quien le escriba*."[7] The contribution of these writers to magical realism and their overriding concern for style and technique has undoubtedly influenced Benet's own writing, as the Latin American new novel continues to gain prestige in contemporary Spanish literature. It must be pointed out, however, that Benet doubts the contention that the Latin American novelists are developing a new literary language in their novels. Although at times his own peripatetic, twisting style suggests a certain reticence concerning the efficacy of language, Benet candidly admits that he possesses complete confidence in the ability of words to express his personal ideas and insights. Consequently, he feels no need to create a "new" language and takes little interest in what he considers to be the insubstantial and somewhat pompous pretensions associated with the "new" language of the Latin American new novel.[8]

José Corrales Egea has suggested that the *contraola* novelists of the late 1960's (of which Benet is an outstanding example) have modeled their writing after the French *nouveau roman*. He claims that Benet (and such other writers as Delibes, Goytisolo and Cela) "ilustran particularmente bien la búsqueda, la mimesis y la servidumbre [del *nouveau roman*]."[9] In the case of Benet,

[7]Juan Benet, "De Canudos a Macondo," *Revista de Occidente*, 2ª Serie, Vol. 24, N° 70 (enero de 1969), 49-57.

[8]Personal interview with Juan Benet, 8 June, 1975.

[9]José Corrales Egea, *La novela española actual* (Madrid: Cuadernos para el Diálogo, 1971), p. 209.

however, Corrales speaks from both a lack of understanding and critical insight. As discussed above, Benet has read extensively in the literature of other countries, but least of all in contemporary French literature. We can discover in his works elements of Faulkner's style, Proust's memory or a general similarity to certain Latin American writers such as Rulfo or Euclides da Cunha. To a certain extent Benet is an eclectic who forthrightly admits that he has been influenced by other authors. However, his novels stand out for their extraordinary complexity and depth of composition and a rarely equaled manipulation of the Spanish language. As José María Alfaro has noted, "¿Existe o no una nueva novela española? Juan Benet da la respuesta afirmativa con su vocación y con su obra."[10]

Only time can confirm Julián Ríos' assertion that Benet and Juan Goytisolo are the two antagonists in the development of a new direction for the Spanish novel. Their influence on other writers and younger generations has yet to be established. However, though the final figure of Benet's carpet can only be determined in the future,[11] it is not premature to conclude that Benet's novels offer a new literary alternative in Spain. Benet can perhaps be regarded most accurately as a novelist's novelist (or a critic's novelist), who writes difficult works of literature for a minority public. We have attempted in the present study to discover several of the elements which make his novels so unique and frequently bewildering. Yet his entire manner of writing does not lend itself to complete understanding, primarily, I believe, because the reality which he creates in his novels defies a logical and rational hermeneutics. As Sergio Gómez Parra has so aptly stated, "De todos modos, respecto a Benet, todo lo que se diga será siempre una aproximación."[12]

---

[10]José María Alfaro, review of *Un viaje de invierno*, *ABC*, 25 de enero de 1973, p. 15.

[11]At the present time (June, 1975), Benet is working on another novel, which he projects will be finished in three or four years. In the fall of 1975 he will publish a collection of essays on literary theory.

[12]Sergio Gómez Parra, p. 12.

BIBLIOGRAPHY

Works by Juan Benet

Novels

Volverás a Región. 2ª ed. Barcelona: Ediciones Destino, 1967.

Una meditación. Barcelona: Seix Barral, 1970.

Una tumba. Barcelona: Editorial Lumen, 1971.

Un viaje de invierno. Barcelona: La Gaya Ciencia, 1972.

La otra casa de Mazón. Barcelona: Seix Barral, 1973.

Short Stories

Nunca llegarás a nada. Madrid: Editorial Tebas, 1961. 2ª ed., Alianza Editorial, 1968.

Cinco narraciones y dos fábulas. Barcelona: La Gaya Ciencia, 1972.

Sub rosa. Barcelona: La Gaya Ciencia, 1973.

Theater

Max. Revista Española, N° 4, 1953.

Teatro. Madrid: Siglo XXI de España Editores, 1971. (*Anastas o el origen de la Constitución*; *Agonía Confutans*; *Un caso de conciencia*)

Essay

La inspiración y el estilo. Madrid: Revista de Occidente, 1966. 2ª ed., Seix Barral, 1974.

Puerta de tierra. Barcelona: Seix Barral, 1970.

Articles and Reviews

"Joseph Heller: *Trampa 22*." Revista de Occidente, 2ª Serie, Vol. 1, N° 2 (mayo de 1963), 247-250.

"Agonía del humor." *Revista de Occidente*, 2ª Serie, Vol. 4, N° 11 (febrero de 1964), 235-241.

"Francisco Candel: los otros catalanes." *Revista de Occidente*, 2ª Serie, Vol. 12, N° 34 (enero de 1966), 117-122.

"Ilusitana." *Revista de Occidente*, 2ª Serie, Vol. 18, N° 54 (septiembre de 1967), 336-352.

"Toledo situado." *Cuadernos Hispanoamericanos*, N° 216 (diciembre de 1967), 571-581.

"La violencia de la posguerra." *Revista de Occidente*, 2ª Serie, Vol. 27, N° 81 (diciembre de 1969), 348-361.

"Cordelia Khan." *Cuadernos Hispanoamericanos*, N° 231 (marzo de 1969), 503-521.

"De Canudos a Macondo." *Revista de Occidente*, 2ª Serie, Vol. 24, N° 70 (enero de 1969), 49-57.

"Cinco respuestas a Proust." *Informaciones de las artes y las letras* (Supplement to *Informaciones*), 10 de julio de 1969, p. 3.

"Contra James Joyce." *Informaciones de las artes y las letras* (Supplement to *Informaciones*), 9 de julio de 1970, pp. 1, 2.

"Samuel Beckett, Premio Nobel, 1969." *Revista de Occidente*, 2ª Serie, Vol. 28, N° 83 (febrero de 1970), 226-230.

"Reflexiones sobre Galdós"; "Mesa redonda sobre la novela"; "Respuesta al Señor Montero." *Cuadernos para el Diálogo*, Número Extraordinario XXIII (diciembre de 1970).

"Los padres." *El Urogallo*, Vol. 1, N° 1 (febrero de 1970), 62-66.

"Los escritores y la edición de libros." *Cuadernos para el Diálogo*, N° 96 (agosto de 1971), 24-25.

"La esferodoxia." *Cuadernos para el Diálogo*, N° 100 (enero de 1972), 102-103.

"El crítico, hombre de orden." *Indice*, N° 301-302 (enero-febrero de 1972), 41-42.

"Barojiana." *Barojiana*. Juan Benet, *et al.* Madrid: Taurus, 1972. pp. 11-45.

"Breve historia de *Volverás a Región*." *Revista de Occidente*, 2ª Serie, Vol. 45, N° 134 (mayo de 1974), 160-165.

"From Madrid, Observations on Military Behavior." Trans.
Barbara Solomon. *The New York Times*, 15 August, 1975,
p. 35.

"Prólogo" to *Palmeras salvajes* by William Faulkner. Trans.
Jorge Luis Borges. Barcelona: E.D.H.A.S.A., 1970.

"Prólogo" to *Industrias y andanzas de Alfanhuí* by Rafael
Sánchez Ferlosio. Barcelona: Salvat, 1970.

"Prólogo" to *El 'Ulises' de James Joyce* by Stuart Gilbert.
Trans. Manuel de la Escalera. Madrid: Siglo XXI de España
Editores, 1971.

Works on Juan Benet

Reviews and Interviews

Alfaro, José María. Review of *Un viaje de invierno*. *ABC*, 25 de
enero de 1973, p. 15.

Anón. "Juan Benet en la Fundación March." *ABC*, 6 de junio de
1975, p. 39.

Azancot, Leopoldo. Review of *Cinco narraciones y dos fábulas*.
El, N° 509 (1973), p. 1212.

Batlló, José. Review of *Volverás a Región*. *Cuadernos Hispanoamericanos*, N° 229 (enero de 1969), 234-237.

Domingo, José. "Del hermetismo al barroco: Juan Benet y Alfonso Grosso." *Insula*, Vol. 29, N° 320-321 (julio-agosto de
1973), p. 20.

——————. Review of *Nunca llegarás a nada*. *Insula*, Vol.
25, N° 278 (enero de 1970), p. 5.

——————. "Otro camino: el de Juan Benet." *Insula*, Vol.
28, N° 312 (noviembre de 1972), p. 6.

——————. Review of *Una meditación*. *Insula*, Vol. 25,
N° 282 (mayo de 1970), p. 7.

Fossey, Jean Michel. "Entrevista con Rafael Conte." *Indice*, N°
354 (1974), 33-38.

Fernández-Braso, Miguel. "Juan Benet: un talento excitado."
De escritor a escritor. Barcelona: Editorial Taber, 1970. pp.
197-203.

Franz, Thomas. Review of *La otra casa de Mazón*. *Journal of Spanish Studies: Twentieth Century*, Vol. 2, No. 2 (Fall, 1973), 197-198.

Gimferrer, Pedro. Review of *Volerás a Región*. *El Ciervo*, N° 179 (1969), p. 15.

Gómez Parra, Sergio. Review of *Una meditación*. *Reseña*, N° 8 (1971), 84-85.

_____. Review of *Una tumba*. *Reseña*, N° 9 (1972), 18-19.

Guelbenzu, José María. "Dos libros de Juan Benet." *Cuadernos para el Diálogo*, N° 73 (octubre de 1969), 48.

Gullón, Ricardo. Review of *Sub rosa*. *Journal of Spanish Studies: Twentieth Century*, Vol. 3, No. 2 (Fall, 1975), 153-154.

Johnson, Roberta. Review of *Sub rosa*. *Books Abroad*. Vol. 48, No. 4 (Autumn, 1974), 743-744.

Marín Morales, J. A. Review of *Puerta de tierra*. *Arbor*, N° 295-296 (julio-agosto de 1970), 135-138.

Núñez, Antonio. "Encuentro con Juan Benet." *Insula*, Vol. 24, N° 269 (abril de 1969), 4.

Quiñonero, Juan Pedro. "Juan Benet: entre la ironía y la destrucción." *Informaciones de las artes y las letras* (Supplement to *Informaciones*), 2 de octubre de 1969, p. 3.

Rico, Eduardo. "Entrevista con Juan Benet." *Triunfo*, 22 de agosto de 1970, p. 2.

Rodríguez Padrón, Jorge. Review of *Cinco narraciones y dos fábulas*. *Camp de L'Arpa: Revista de Literatura*, N° 7 (octubre de 1973), 37-38.

Sordo, Enrique. Review of *Un viaje de invierno*. *El*, N° 502 (1972), p. 1108.

Soto Verges, Rafael. Review of *La inspiración y el estilo*. *Cuadernos Hispanoamericanos*, N° 209 (mayo de 1967), 446-449.

Urbina, Pedro Antonio. Review of *Un viaje de invierno*. *Indice*, N° 310 (1 de julio de 1972), 25.

Studies

Carenas, Francisco and José Ferrando. "El mundo pre-perceptivo de *Volverás a Región*." *La sociedad española en la novela de la postguerra*. New York: Eliseo Torres & Sons, 1971. pp. 171-192.

Conte, Rafael. "Juan Benet, o una metáfora de la destrucción." *Informaciones de las artes y las letras* (Supplement to *Informaciones*), 28 de mayo de 1970, p. 3.

Corrales Egea, José. *La novela española actual*. Madrid: Cuadernos para el Diálogo, 1971.

Durán, Manuel. "Juan Benet y la nueva novela española." *Cuadernos Americanos*, Vol. 195, N° 4 (julio-agosto de 1974), 193-205.

Gimferrer, Pedro. "En torno a *Volverás a Región*." *Insula*, Vol. 24, N° 226 (enero de 1969), 14.

_____. "Sobre Juan Benet." *Plural*, N° 17 (febrero de 1973), 13-16.

Gómez Parra, Sergio. "Juan Benet: la ruptura de un horizonte novelístico." *Reseña*, N° 9 (1972), 3-12.

Guillermo, Edenia and Juana Amelia Hernández. *La novelística española de los sesenta*. New York: Eliseo Torres & Sons, 1971.

Gullón, Ricardo. "Esperando a Coré." *Revista de Occidente*, 2ª Serie, Vol. 49, N° 145 (abril de 1975), 16-36.

_____. "Una región laberíntica que bien pudiera llamarse España." *Insula*, Vol. 29, N° 319 (junio de 1973), pp. 3, 10.

Literatura de España día a día: 1970-1971. Ed. Antonio Iglesias Laguna. Madrid: Editora Nacional, 1972.

Marco, Joaquín. "Las obras recientes de Juan Benet." *Nueva literatura en España y América*. Barcelona: Editorial Lumen, 1972. pp. 143-155.

Oliart, Alberto. "Viaje a Región." *Revista de Occidente*, 2ª Serie, Vol. 27, N° 80 (noviembre de 1970), 224-234.

Ortega, José. "Estudios sobre la obra de Juan Benet." *Cuadernos Hispanoamericanos*, N° 284 (febrero de 1974), 229-258.

Rodríguez Padrón, Jorge. "Volviendo a Región." *Camp de L'Arpa: Revista de Literatura*, N° 7 (octubre de 1973), 37-38.

Sanz Villanueva, Santos. *Tendencias de la novela española actual*. Madrid: Cuadernos para el Diálogo, 1972.

170

Sobejano, Gonzalo. *Novela española de nuestro tiempo*. Madrid: Editorial Prensa Española, 1970.

Villanueva, Darío. "La novela de Juan Benet." *Camp de L'Arpa: Revista de Literatura*, N° 8 (noviembre de 1973), 9-16.

Other Works Cited

Aiken, Conrad. "William Faulkner: The Novel as Form." *Faulkner: Four Decades of Criticism*. Ed. Linda W. Wagner. East Lansing: Michigan State University Press. Pp. 134-140.

Beck, Warren. "William Faulkner's Style." *Faulkner: Four Decades of Criticism*. Ed. Linda W. Wagner. East Lansing: Michigan State University Press, 1973. Pp. 141-154.

Booth, Wayne C. *The Rhetoric of Fiction*. Chicago & London: University of Chicago Press, 1970.

Borges, Jorge Luis. *Discusión*. 5ª ed. Buenos Aires: Emecé, 1969.

Butor, Michel. *L'Emploi du Temps*. Paris: Les Editions de Minuit, 1957.

Buckley, Ramón. *Problemas formales en la novela española actual*. Barcelona: Ediciones Península, 1968.

Castellet, J. M., Pere Gimferrer and Julián Ríos. "Encuesta: Nueva literatura española." *Plural*, N° 25 (octubre de 1973), 4-7.

Coleridge, Samuel T. "Bibliographia Literaria." *Complete Works of S. T. Coleridge*. New York: Harper & Brothers, 1868.

Domingo, José. *La novela española del siglo XX*. Barcelona: Editorial Labor, 1973.

Faulkner, William. Review of *Test Pilot* by Jimmy Collins. *The American Mercury*, 36 (1935), 370-372.

Ferreras, Juan Ignacio. *Tendencias de la novela española actual*. Paris: Ediciones Hispanoamericanas, 1970.

Freud, Sigmund. *An Outline of Psycho-Analysis*. Trans. James Strachy. New York: W. W. Norton, 1969.

García-Viñó, M. "Por una nueva novela." *Arbor*, Vol. 88, N° 342 (junio de 1974), 133-137.

Gil Casado, Pablo. *La novela social española*. Barcelona: Seix Barral, 1968.

Goytisolo, Juan. *El furgón de cola*. Paris: Ruedo Ibérico, 1967.

_____. "La novela española contemporánea." *Libre*, N° 2 (diciembre, enero, febrero, 1971-1972), 33-40.

Iglesias Laguna, Antonio. *Treinta años de la novela española*. Madrid: Editorial Prensa Española, 1969.

Joad, C. E. M. *Guide to Philosophy*. New York: Dover Publications, 1946.

Kawin, Bruce F. *Telling It Again and Again*. Ithaca & London: Cornell University Press, 1972.

Luis Leal. "El realismo mágico en la literatura hispanoamericana." *Cuadernos Americanos*, Año 26, Vol. 153, N° 4 (julio-agosto de 1967), 230-235.

"Le 'nouveau roman' Espagnol." *Les Lettres Français*, 19 juillet, 1962, pp. 4-7.

Marcuse, Herbert. *Eros and Civilization*. Boston: Beacon Press, 1966.

Marías, Julián. *Ortega: Circunstancia y vocación*. Madrid: Revista de Occidente, 1960.

_____. "Prólogo" to *La novelística de Camilo José Cela* by Paul Ilie. Madrid: Gredos, 1959.

Mendilow, A. A. *Time and the Novel*. New York: Humanities Press, 1965.

Minney, R. J. *Rasputin*. New York: David McKay Co., 1973.

Nora, Eugenio G. de. *La novela española contemporánea*. 2ª ed. 3 vols. Madrid: Gredos, 1970.

Ortega y Gasset, José. *Obras completas*. Madrid: Revista de Occidente, 1973.

Poe, Edgar Allan. "The Philosophy of Composition." *Works*. Vol. I. New York & London: Funk and Wagnalls, 1904.

Ponce de León, José Luis. *La novela española de la guerra civil*. Madrid: Insula, 1971.

Richards, I. A. *The Philosophy of Rhetoric*. New York & London: Oxford University Press, 1936.

Robbe-Grillet, Alain. *For a New Novel*. 2nd ed. Trans. Richard

Howard. New York: Grove Press, 1965.

Rogers, B. G. *Proust's Narrative Technique*. Geneva: Librairie Droz, 1965.

Sartre, Jean-Paul. "Existentialism." *Existentialism from Dostoevsky to Sartre*. Ed. Walter Kaufmann. Cleveland & New York: World Publishing Co., 1956. Pp. 222-311.

_____. "Time in Faulkner: *The Sound and the Fury*." Trans. Martine Darmon. *Faulkner: Three Decades of Criticism*. Ed. Frederick J. Hoffman and Olga W. Vickery. New York: Harcourt, Brace & World, 1963. Pp. 225-232.

Slatoff, Walter. "The Edge of Order: The Pattern of Faulkner's Rhetoric." *Faulkner: Four Decades of Criticism*. Ed. Linda Wagner. East Lansing: Michigan State University Press, 1973. Pp. 155-179.

Sontag, Susan. *Against Interpretation*. New York: Dell, 1970.

Stanford, W. B. *Greek Metaphor*. Oxford: B. Blackwell, 1936.

Strange, G. Robert. "Introduction" to *The History of Henry Edmond* by William Makepeace Thackeray. New York: Holt, Rinehart & Winston, 1962.

Swiggart, Peter. *The Art of Faulkner's Novels*. Austin: University of Texas Press, 1967.

Vickery, Olga. *The Novels of William Faulkner*. Baton Rouge: Lousiana State University Press, 1964.

Vilanova, Antonio. "De la objetividad al subjetivismo en la novela española actual." *Prosa novelesca actual*. Universidad Internacional Menéndez Pelayo, 1967.

Vivas, Eliseo. *Creation and Discovery*. New York: Noonday Press, 1955.

INDEX